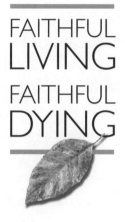

FAITHFUL
LIVING

FAITHFUL
DYING

End of Life Task Force

Standing Commission on National Concerns

General Convention of the Episcopal Church

Members of the task force:

Cynthia B. Cohen, Ph.D., J.D., Chair

The Rev. Randolph K. Dales

The Rev. Jan C. Heller, Ph.D.

Bruce Jennings, M.A.

Margaret E. Mohrmann, M.D., Ph.D.

The Rev. E. F. Michael Morgan, Ph.D.

The Rt. Rev. Kenneth L. Price, D.D.

The Rev. David A. Scott, Ph.D.

Timothy F. Sedgwick, Ph.D.

David H. Smith, Ph.D.

Karen Roberts Turner, J.D., M.A.

FAITHFUL LIVING

FAITHFUL DYING

ANGLICAN REFLECTIONS ON END OF LIFE CARE

Cynthia B. Cohen

Jan C. Heller

Bruce Jennings

E. F. Michael Morgan

David A. Scott

Timothy F. Sedgwick

David H. Smith

MOREHOUSE PUBLISHING

Morehouse Publishing
P.O. Box 1321
Harrisburg, PA 17105

Morehouse Publishing is a division of The Morehouse Group.

Printed in the United States of America

Cover design by Kirk Bingaman

ISBN 0-8192-1830-8

Library of Congress Cataloging-in-Publication Data
Faithful living, faithful dying : Anglican reflections on end of life care / Cynthia B. Cohen ... [et al.].
        p.   cm.
    Includes bibliographical references.
    ISBN 0-8192-1830-8 (pbk. : alk. paper) .
    1. Terminally ill—Miscellanea. 2. Death—Religious aspects—Episcopal Church.
    3. Death—Moral and ethical aspects. 4. Medical ethics. I. Cohen, Cynthia B.
    R726.8 .F34 2000
    174'.24—dc21   99-085980

First Edition
3 5 7 9 10 8 6 4

So may'st thou live, till like ripe Fruit thou drop
Into thy Mother's lap, or be with ease
Gather'd, not harshly pluckt, for death mature

John Milton, *Paradise Lost,* Book XI.535–538

CONTENTS

ACKNOWLEDGMENTS

The task force would like to express its gratitude to the late Rev. Dr. Charles Price, Professor Emeritus, Virginia Theological Seminary, Alexandria, Virginia, who died shortly after this book was written, for his presentation on the implications of the liturgy for those making difficult decisions near the end of life. As he reminded us, death does not have the last word. We would also like to extend our thanks to Joanne Lynn, M.D., Director of the Center to Improve the Care of the Dying, George Washington University, Washington, D.C., for addressing us about ethical and medical concerns surrounding care for those near the end of life.

The task force is highly appreciative of the work of Elizabeth Leibold McCloskey, M.A.R., of Falls Church, Virginia, who provided editorial suggestions and perspicacious comments about several drafts of this book.

We also express thanks to the following persons for responding to our request for materials and comments related to issues that arise for parishioners and priests surrounding death and dying.

The Rev. Carol M. Arney, Christ Church Episcopal, Kealakekua, Hawaii
The Rev. Canon Noel A. Bailey, St. George's Episcopal Church, Lee, Massachusetts
Jean Ball, Esq., Fairfax, Virginia
The Rev. Robert Bruckart, Director of Pastoral Care, Holmes Regional Medical Center, Melbourne, Florida
The Rev. Charles F. Brumbaugh, The Church of Ascension and Holy Trinity, Cincinnati, Ohio
The Rt. Rev. Richard S.O. Chang, Bishop of Hawaii, Honolulu, Hawaii
The Rev. Peter Coffin, St. Paul's Episcopal Church, Lancaster, New Hampshire
The Rev. D. Lorne Coyle, Trinity Church, Vero Beach, Florida
The Rev. Charles T. Crane, Rector Emeritus, Church of the Holy Trinity, Diocese of Hawaii, Mesa, Arizona
Dr. Louie Crew, Newark, New Jersey

The Rev. Jean Denton, National Episcopal Health Ministries,
St. Paul's Episcopal Church, Indianapolis, Indiana
The Rev. Stephen Elkins-Williams, Chapel of the Cross, Chapel Hill,
North Carolina
Georgette Forney, The National Organization of Episcopalians for Life,
Sewickley, Pennsylvania
The Rev. Sharline A. Fulton, Assistant to the Bishop of Pennsylvania and
Adjunct Priest, St. Martin-in-the-Fields Church, Chestnut Hill,
Pennsylvania
The Rev. Steve Gehrig, St. Margaret's Episcopal Church, Bellevue,
Washington
The Rev. Edward Stone Gleason, Editor and Director, Forward
Movement Publications, Cincinnati, Ohio
The Rev. Dr. Arthur Hadley, St. John's Episcopal Church, Worthington,
Ohio
The Rev. Muffy Harmon, Cathedral Church of St. Paul, Des Moines, Iowa
The Rt. Rev. Donald P. Hart, Assistant Bishop, Diocese of Southern
Virginia, Petersburg, Virginia
C. E. Hawtry, M.D., Iowa City, Iowa
Joan C. Irving, Patient Representative, Gwinnett Hospital System,
Lawrenceville, Georgia
The Rev. Peter Kalunian, St. Paul's Episcopal Church, Kennewick,
Washington
Carl Knirk, Office of Planned Giving, Diocese of Olympia, Seattle,
Washington
The Rev. Michael Kreutzer, St. Mark's Episcopal Church, Dayton, Ohio
Catherine Loveland, Affirmative Aging Commission, Diocese of
Southern Ohio
The Rev. Martin F. McCarthy, St. John's Episcopal Church, Charlotte,
North Carolina
The Rev. David O. McCoy, Pickerington, Ohio
The Rev. Dorian McGlannan, Church of the Good Shepherd, Federal
Way, Washington
The Rev. Portia Mather-Hempler, St. Andrew's Episcopal Church,
Saratoga, California
The Rev. J. Hollis Maxson, Honolulu, Hawaii
Peter M. Norman, Episcopal Retirement Homes, Diocese of Southern
Ohio, Cincinnati, Ohio
The Rev. Roderick Pierce, Chaplain, St. Luke's Episcopal Hospital,
Houston, Texas
The Rev. Greg Rickel, St. Peter's Episcopal Church, Conway, Arkansas
The Rev. Canon Anne W. Robbins, St. Patrick's Episcopal Church,
Dublin, Ohio

The Rev. Janna Roche, Charlottesville, Virginia

The Rt. Rev. Calvin O. Schofield, Bishop of Southeast Florida, Miami, Florida

Edwina M. Simpson, Planned Giving, The Episcopal Church Foundation, Dearborn, Michigan

The Rev. Joanne L. Skidmore, St. Matthias Episcopal Church, Waukesha, Wisconsin

The Rev. Charles H. Stacey and the Good Grief Group, St. Mark's-in-the-Valley Episcopal Church, Los Olivos, California

Sandol Stoddard, Holualoa, Hilo, Hawaii

James C. Taylor, Las Vegas, Nevada

The Rev. Dr. Joseph W. Trigg, Christ Church, La Plata, Maryland

The Rev. Patrick T. Twomey, All Saints Episcopal Church, Appleton, Wisconsin

The Rev. Regina Volpe, Vitas Hospice Care, Chicagoland West Program, Chicago, Illinois

The Rev. Dr. Francis H. Wade, St. Alban's Church, Washington, D.C.

The Rev. Dr. Timothy West, Chillicothe, Ohio

Anne Moats Williams, Diocese of Iowa, Anamosa, Iowa

The Rev. Heather Buchanan Wiseman, St. Andrew's Episcopal Church, Cincinnati, Ohio

The Rev. Dolores W. Witt, Chaplain, Canterbury Court, West Carrollton, Ohio

INTRODUCTION

Life is too short and death goes on forever—or so we are taught by our society. Consequently, many of us struggle to cram as much as we can into our lives, fearing that death will take them from us at some unexpected moment. When illness strikes, we reach out eagerly for new medical technologies that give us the power to extend our lives much longer than our grandparents ever dreamed of living. Respirators, heart-lung machines, "miracle" drugs, and organ transplants, we are led to believe, promise to keep us alive forever. Many of us embrace them in a struggle to avoid death at any cost.

But as Christians, we know at a deeper level that our society has it all backwards. It is not that life ends and that death goes on forever. Death is but a single event that is not itself the last word. At the heart of Christian faith is the Easter story of the Resurrection revealing that God does not abandon us at death, but raises us to new life. Nothing, Paul declares, can separate us from the love of God, "neither death, nor life, nor angels, nor rulers, nor things present, nor things to come, nor powers, nor height, nor depth, nor anything else in all creation" (Romans 8:38). When we acknowledge this deeper truth, we recognize that our struggle is not to remain alive forever at any cost, but to live faithfully and to die faithfully.

Faithful living calls us to cherish mortal human life as we know it. The words of Moses admonishing the people of Israel to choose life present one of the basic tenets of faithful living: we are to love and hold onto life. Thus, when illness strikes, faithful living leads us to seek out medical assistance and to pray for a return to health. Yet faithful living also requires us to recognize that we cannot fend off aging and mortality forever. The call to cherish life is a steadfast hope that we hold in the face of the reality that eventually and inevitably we will die.

The shape and duration of our dying, however, has been changed drastically by medical advances during the last generation, especially in the United States and the developed world. Medical machinery can now compensate for failing organ systems. Powerful medicines can control blood pressure, fluid levels, and body chemistry. Life processes can be sustained and prolonged through artificial means for extra weeks, months, and even years. In the past, our immediate response to the threat of death was to declare, "Do everything that you can, doctor!" This seems a less obvious directive to our professional caregivers today in the face of our invasive and often burdensome medical powers. If medical technology had the power to cure and to restore human function fully, then a request for the medical extension of our lives would be an obvious expression of faithful living. But too often we see that this technology has only the power to sustain life processes without returning patients to a condition that has meaning and dignity. When this is the case, we are called to recognize this, emotionally difficult as it may be, and, living faithfully, to move toward faithful dying.

Medical advances, however, often mask the reality of human mortality, challenging us to expand our notion of who is dying and to develop more appropriate ways of caring for them. We currently fashion care at the end of life exclusively on the classical model of "terminal illness," according to which a person looks terribly sick, is bedridden, and is known to have very little time left to live—a few days to a few months. This model allows us to avoid the distressing realization that there are other persons who will also die within the foreseeable future but will take somewhat longer to reach the point of death. These individuals suffer from chronic and debilitating illnesses that will take their lives more slowly over a period of months or even years. They will not go through a discrete period of dying and then abruptly die. In the course of their illnesses, some among them will experience intermittent downward swings and will be "rescued" in repeated sequences, emerging at ever-lower plateaus of functioning, until finally they can be "rescued" no longer. Others will die slowly and steadily, gradually moving into the advanced stages of a condition that has no clear terminal phase. Our societal unwillingness to accept that we will die leads us to deny as a community that persons in these straits are headed toward death. As a consequence, we refuse to acknowledge that they, too, need special end-of-life care.

The awareness of death as a part of life is a significant strand of Christian thought about the meaning of faithful living and faithful dying. There is an urgent need today to reaffirm and accept this strand as we address the many difficult questions that arise for those near the end of life. First among these are the difficult questions of what it means to be dying and when medical intervention for those approaching death should cease. Troubling questions arise again and again in individual circumstances. When, if ever, are we called to stop the use of a respirator and let my grandmother die? Should we provide artificial nutrition and hydration for my best friend until the last possible moment? From which of his multiple conditions—heart disease, dementia, kidney failure—should my father be allowed to die? When a dying person can no longer participate in answering these questions, the responses to them become even more difficult and agonizing for those tending to that person.

A second set of questions emerges from our consciousness of death as a part of life. What must we offer to the dying to allow them to live well in their remaining days, in right relation with their family, friends, and God? How can we help them to die faithfully in peace and comfort, surrounded by a nurturing community? Can pain control for them ever be excessive? Is it wrong to end their lives directly if they are in terrible pain and suffering? How can we restructure our healthcare system so that it offers adequate and appropriate care to those who are dying? These concerns are informed most fundamentally by how we understand our lives in relationship with God, what that requires, and what that enables in our living and our dying. They are drawn together by the question: What do faithful living and faithful dying mean today as we near life's end?

We do not care adequately for the living unless we address the difficult issues surrounding death and dying and then offer ways in which to prepare faithfully for them. And we do not care adequately for the dying—who are still living—unless we provide them with love, support, and palliation, whether they will die in a few months or at a somewhat more distant time.

Within this larger context, the General Convention of the Episcopal Church has asked for guidance on these matters. In a 1997 resolution, it called for the creation of a working group to:

> study the theological and ethical implications of end of life issues, including adequate palliative care, euthanasia, and assisted suicide, taking into consideration pertinent studies in the Christian moral perspective, such as the "Washington Report" [*Assisted Suicide and Euthanasia: Christian Moral Perspectives*],[1] previous resolutions of the General Convention,[2] and recent Supreme Court decisions.[3]

The End of Life Task Force was formed in response to that resolution. In this book, members of this task force address a broad range of issues that are generated by the need to provide loving and fitting care for those approaching death.

The Episcopal Church has not had many reliable means for developing moral teachings that would:

- inform the conscience of its members in relating Christian faith to decisions regarding care near the end of life;
- present the reasons behind the understandings of the Church concerning care near the end of life set out in General Convention resolutions;
- provide resources that support those making difficult moral decisions about the use of medical treatment near the end of life; and

• address the larger public by identifying important moral issues related to care near the end of life that call for changes in public policy. The Church has largely developed resolutions at General Convention to legislate what the Church and its members should believe and do and how society should respond to difficult moral issues. A rush to legislate by means of resolutions, however, is likely to politicize and divide the Church into those for and against certain proposals. Sometimes these resolutions have been accompanied by reports seeking to summarize contemporary understandings of an issue. Yet such reports have often been limited as teaching documents: limited in length, further limited by time constraints and budget, and even further limited at times by the special interests of the committee or commission writing them.

This End of Life Task Force has been blessed with the opportunity and challenge to do something different. What distinguishes it is not that it is a committee charged with representing a variety of specific interests, but that it is a working group of persons who, as its enabling resolution states, provide "a wide range of expertise and approaches to medicine, ethics, and theology." It is a "working group" in that it does not claim the authority to give final answers to pressing questions that can arise for Christians near the end of life but is working toward finding them. Although it hopes it has achieved a *consensus fidelium,* an understanding that can be shared in common by the faithful, it sees itself playing a more modest role as an exploratory body attempting to carry further conversations already in progress. These conversations encompass difficult issues and hard questions that can lead to ambiguity and division. To avoid these untoward results, the End of Life Task Force has striven to honor the consciences of individuals as they are informed by the Christian faith, offering understandings from our inherited Christian moral tradition and from contemporary discussion of matters of death and dying.

We recognize that the Anglican Communion is a worldwide fellowship of Christian churches that are nurtured by different cultural traditions and that a variety of ethnic and cultural treasures can be found within the Episcopal Church. Some cultural traditions may have a different understanding from that of the predominant Western one about such matters as whether to tell those who are dying the truth about their condition or what it means to provide nutrition for those who are near the end of life. They may therefore take a different approach from that of their Western brothers and sisters to the appropriateness of obtaining informed consent or to the use of artificial nutrition and hydration. We also recognize that the Anglican Communion is united by "one Lord, one Faith, one Baptism" (BCP, 299) and that the Church community provides a context of shared wisdom and mutual accountability in which distinctive cultures can flourish. We therefore acknowledge the need to respect the deeply held views of

persons from cultural traditions other than the one immediately surrounding us and to attempt to incorporate their views into conversations
about end-of-life matters within the Anglican tradition.

The focus of this book is on the pressing, underlying end-of-life issues
that the Church faces today. It therefore provides an updated theological,
ethical, pastoral, liturgical, and policy discussion for the Church as a
whole, for individuals in their own lives and consciences, for professionals
such as clergy and healthcare providers, and for those who make public
policy. This book is meant to be used hand-in-hand with another book
that addresses end-of-life issues from the perspective of individuals making healthcare decisions and family and friends who care for them. This
second, case-based companion book, *Toward a Good Christian Death:
Crucial Treatment Choices*, was developed by the Committee on Medical
Ethics of the Diocese of Washington.[4] The two books together are
designed for use by bodies of the Church, diocesan and parish groups,
clerical and seminary classes, individual Episcopalians, public policy makers, and those of other religious traditions or of no religious tradition who
have an interest in discussions of end-of-life matters within the Christian
community.

In the present book, we articulate how Christian faith informs a
Christian response to those who are approaching death and to those who
care for them. Part I presents characteristic Anglican theological and ethical understandings as these illumine faithful living and faithful dying. Part
II offers ways in which these understandings shape Christian responses to
the ethical questions, spiritual concerns, pastoral issues, liturgical needs,
and public policy matters that arise near the end of life. It explores the
interconnections between these understandings and the concrete choices
that must be made near the end of life from the perspectives of individual
persons facing death and those caring for them, local congregations, the
Church-at-large, healthcare organizations, and public policy makers.

Chapter 1, "The Reality of Death," delves into our apprehensions about
death and dying, noting two basic meanings that death has for us and how
these shape the ways in which Christians confront the questions and pressing needs that emerge at the end of life today. The following chapter, "God,
Death, and Anglican Theology," views death as a critical point that offers
opportunities to deepen our relationship with God and to overcome our
tendency to idolize the limited and perishable goods of this world. It sees
the Anglican tradition as marked not only by a set of beliefs, but also by a
way of life that flows from these beliefs that is sacramental, evangelical,
theocentric, incarnational, and corporate. Part I concludes with Chapter 3,
"Moral Journey, Ethical Compass," in which the task force offers a distinctive vision of how the Christian way of life informs ethical discernment as
we near death. To this end, it articulates three themes: that care at the end

of life calls for the responsible use of human power; it calls for right relationships among persons; and it calls for relationships, resources, and empowerment that promote human good.

Having described in Part I a Christian framework for understanding death and our obligations in the face of it, the task force turns in Part II to explore how this theological and moral vision can be brought to bear on the experience of dying today. Chapter 4, "Using Our Medical Powers Appropriately," addresses several of the more pressing ethical issues that arise for individuals near the end of life and for those caring for them, in view of the unprecedented control over the time and manner of our deaths that contemporary medical technology brings. The task force rejects as idolatrous a vitalism that contends that medicine must keep people alive as long as possible. It then addresses several difficult ethical issues: whether we are morally required to provide such life-sustaining treatments as artificial feeding to those near death, the role of hospice and moral queries about appropriate use of pain-relieving drugs for those approaching death, and whether physician-assisted suicide is a practice we should embrace. A closely related chapter, "Making Responsible Treatment Choices," follows, which takes as its foundation our right and responsibility as Christians to make healthcare choices. In it, the task force considers the question of whether it is always best to seek and tell the truth within the doctor-patient relationship, the advantages and drawbacks of developing advance directives for end-of-life care, and modes of making medical care decisions for those who cannot decide for themselves.

The role of congregations as the primary locus of Christian life and teaching is captured in Chapter 6, "Accepting, Caring, and Mourning." This chapter underscores the ways that Christians in community can help parishioners accept the reality that we will die, care for those who are near death, and comfort those who mourn. Chapter 7 explores ways in which the church-at-large can enrich its response to ordained and lay ministers in the face of shifts in their roles due to changes in the healthcare climate and the circumstances of those approaching death. It goes on to recommend ways in which our liturgies can be expanded and new liturgies developed to respond more adequately to the needs of those who face dying in these changed circumstances. Chapter 8, "Broadening the Conversation," addresses the challenge that the lack of adequate palliative care for those near death presents to us as a society. It recommends steps that the Episcopal Church can take to articulate a moral vision for health care near the end of life that it can bring to the attention of healthcare professionals, healthcare organizations, and public policy makers.

In "Final Reflections," the task force pulls together its recommendations as they apply to individual patients and those close to them, congregations, the church-at-large, and public servants. It goes on to explain and assess the way in which it has proceeded and to suggest ways in which the Church can develop moral teachings on controversial issues in the future. Useful materials for congregations are drawn together in the appendix, including a wealth of information about preparing for death, keeping company with the dying, making burial arrangements, using columbariums, and going through mourning. It also includes a service for the time when life-sustaining treatment is withdrawn.

This book is intended as a teaching document to enrich discussion within the Anglican tradition and among others interested in the difficult questions about care at the end of life that arise out of contemporary medical and social realities. We hope that it will become a new and constructive initiative in the life of the Church and will lead to the development of effective teaching materials for its members, other Christians, and interested persons. We dare to hope further that those who dread dying and those who wonder whether they can muster the courage to care for the dying on their final journey will find this book a source of strength and illumination.

---

1. Committee on Medical Ethics, Episcopal Diocese of Washington, *Assisted Suicide and Euthanasia: Christian Moral Perspectives* (Harrisburg, Pa.: Morehouse, 1997).

2. These are collected in the appendix of Committee on Medical Ethics, Episcopal Diocese of Washington, *Toward a Good Christian Death: Crucial Treatment Choices* (Harrisburg, Pa.: Morehouse, 1999).

3. *Washington v. Glucksberg,* 117 S. Ct. 2258 (1997); *Vacco v. Quill,* 117 S. Ct. 2293 (1997).

4. Committee on Medical Ethics, *Toward a Good Christian Death.*

CHAPTER I

THE REALITY OF DEATH

Death, for Christians, is understood not merely as an event that we must undergo at the end of life but also as an ever-present accompaniment to the story of our lives. It is an integral part of life, a mystery to be contemplated as we live. Here we consider the awesome force of death, exploring the import of the realization that we will die for all of us, but especially for those within the Anglican tradition. We then turn to consider the significance of death as a specific event in our lives. For Christians, the actual experience of death is real, but not ultimate; it does not speak the last word about our human condition. This exploration of the significance of death is not merely a philosophical bypath or theological nicety but is forced upon us by the often difficult decisions—medical, ethical, personal, and spiritual—that we must make when death appears on the horizon. Therefore, the task force reflects here upon how the Anglican perspective on the meaning of death can illuminate the concerns and realities that we face today near the end of life.

DEATH AS A PART OF LIFE

Throughout our lives, especially as we grow older, we are aware that someday we will die. This awareness is not often conscious but lies just beneath the surface, ready to emerge again and again. Many things can call it to mind. The death of someone whom we know well and love reminds us that we, too, must die. The death of a person our own age makes us pause, abruptly bringing our own mortality into focus. News headlines of a massacre, a plane crash, an epidemic, or an accident bring our awareness of the inevitability of our own death rushing to the fore. Even the change of the seasons reminds us that our lives, like all life around us, are caught up in a cycle of birth, growth, decline, and death. Aging makes the reality of upcoming death even more vivid to us as time becomes etched in the lines on our skin. We feel our mortality in our bones and in our discernibly diminishing capacities.

Thus, the awareness that someday we will die accompanies us throughout our lives, waiting to step out of the shadows of our absorption in the activities of daily life. And, in the Christian understanding of death, this is not a bad thing. We are taught by these recurring reminders of death to "number our days," that is, to contemplate that our lives have a limit. We have but one life to live and one life to offer. We can resist this awareness or we can consent to it. For Christians, the awareness of death can be a spiritual discipline, a part of the schooling that teaches us to mature in our faith. Indeed, within the Anglican tradition, a consciousness of the fact that we will die someday is a necessary accompaniment to faithful living.

Yet we receive little support from contemporary society for our Christian endeavor to face death in life. Our culture conspires against acknowledging its inevitability. Death in our secular society typically provokes fear and denial, rather than contemplation and reflection. And so our society deals with death by evasions and lies. Advertisements abound for products promising to hide or remove the signs of aging. Older persons who are approaching death are concealed behind the walls of institutions whose corridors we grace as little as common decency allows. The words "died" and "death" do not pass our lips; we speak instead of someone "passing away" or of "losing" those we love. We flee from acknowledging the reality of death.

Even as our culture conceals death in a heavy cloak of silence, it is obsessed with death. This is because it recognizes it as a power that is out of our control, one for which we have no effective response. To keep death at bay, we treat it as if it is only a fantasy played out in wars in distant lands or a fictional focus of entertainment for us in "gun 'em down" movies, killer video games, and horror houses at Halloween. Death is, for us, an unmentionable subject and yet a source of endless fascination. Our denial of its reality in modern Western culture is, paradoxically, heightened by our refusal to let go of it. Thus, death retains its terrible importance and meaning for us even as we pretend to ignore it.

Commentators have described our culture as "death-denying." Death and dying, this culture teaches, are unspoken terrors that will make their appearance at some far-off time. Therefore, we need not think about them today. It has become more difficult to acknowledge explicitly the reality of death in our society because we press it into a medical model, reducing it to a merely biological problem. Our culture has "assigned" such biological problems to medical experts whose training has taught them to see decline and death as signs of malfunctioning, and finally nonfunctioning, organ systems. Thus, death becomes an untoward biological accident that medicine, with its technological prowess, must attempt to avert. In such ways, our society brackets our awareness of death as an essential part of the story of our lives and makes it increasingly difficult for us to have a "death of our own."[1]

True, there has been a relatively recent movement in Western societies urging an increased awareness of death. A drive toward consumer awareness is one piece of this movement. This drive is designed to help us protect ourselves from exploitation at a particularly vulnerable moment in our lives—the time when we purchase professional services related to dying and death.[2] Such consumer protection requires us to acknowledge at some level, no matter how far removed, that we will die. Another piece of this contemporary death awareness movement is found in alternative, or holistic, medicine, a growing field that appears in part to be a reaction to the dominant medical model of illness, dying, and death. The holistic approach, which views the person as a whole being of mind, body, and spirit, counters our cultural tendency to perceive those who are sick merely as malfunctioning organisms. In so doing, it opens the door to the recognition that, as whole human beings, we are mortal.

The patients' rights movement of recent years provides yet another facet of this thrust toward death awareness, as it calls for respect for patient autonomy and choice in healthcare decisions, especially for those near the end of life. To have the responsibility of making difficult choices about our own treatment is to be forced to face the reality that some therapeutic options will be ineffective and end in death. Still another factor creating greater consciousness of death today is the growth of novel psychological programs that paint dying and death as opportunities for creative self-expression. They direct their clients' energy toward such projects as planning their own pre-death funerals, celebrated while they are still alive, or creating unique forms of ceremonial body disposal on land, sea, and air. Clearly, in order to make arrangements to "die with style," we must face the fact that we are dying.

Although this death awareness movement opens us to the reality of death and dying in some of its manifestations, it fails to capture the dread and loss that death conveys for most people in our society. The medicalization of death overlooks that death is not a mere biological accident. It is an event that overtakes us while we are living, creating in us mixed reactions of fear, love, dread, hope, and flight, long before the event itself arrives. The contemporary drives for consumer awareness and patients' rights, with their focus on protecting and empowering patients in the here and now, seem to disregard this awesome and often terrifying power of our awareness of death. Moreover, a danger of contemporary programs that seek out creative ways of dealing with dying is that they add yet another burden for us to bear. For if our lives are not right in the first place, dying "in character" and "with style" will not be a nurturing act that heightens our awareness of death but a fruitless effort to conform to a frivolous standard that conceals the full reality of death.

In the passive acquiescence of our society to the concealment of death, not only death is being denied. Life also is being denied. We deny that death is an indissoluble part of our lives. We deny the meaning of human life and of human dignity, framed as they are by the reality that, as mortal beings, we can choose to live bravely and faithfully in the face of death. Finally, we deny that we are bound to one another in community by our common mortality and vulnerability. As a result, there is a profound disequilibrium in the way that our society approaches death that, in turn, creates a deep imbalance in the way that it approaches life.

As Christians, we find that an awareness of the certainty of death is uniquely important throughout our lives, an integral part of faithful living. The Bible speaks of death utterly factually, forcing us to recognize our mortality. The reality of death is an unavoidable focus of Christianity, whose Savior, standing at the center of Christian faith and trust, suffered death. The Christian conviction of resurrection underscores the call to accept the inevitability of death, even while affirming that it is not the final word about human life. *The Book of Common Prayer* of the Anglican Communion offers a rich liturgical tradition that sets death within the framework of God's creating, reconciling, and redeeming work. On Ash Wednesday, we engage in preparation for death when ashes are imposed on our foreheads with the words, "Remember that you are dust, and to dust you shall return" (BCP, 265). Our prayers for the ministration to the sick recognize that death is one of the possible outcomes of illness (BCP, 458, 461). In the burial service, we are reminded that "In the midst of life we are in death" (BCP, 484). The reality of death has always been embedded in the consciousness of Christians in such ways.

In earlier centuries, paintings of saints revealed that some kept a human skull among their daily possessions and even placed it before them when they meditated. Macabre as that may seem to our modern sensibilities, such a practice emphasized the truth of their mortality, a truth that no amount of frenetic busyness could eradicate from their awareness. Such an intentional reminder of the reality of death in the midst of life helped these Christians to understand that faithful dying is as much a part of the Christian pilgrimage as faithful living.

Jeremy Taylor, an Anglican divine of the seventeenth century, wrote what has subsequently been recognized as a classic on preparation for death, *The Rule and Exercise of Holy Dying*.[3] It begins with "Reflections on the Vanity and Shortness of Man's Life," in which Taylor compares the world to a storm in which our human lives rise up in each generation like bubbles. Although some lives last longer than others, they all disappear, giving place to others. In this context, Taylor recalls the New Testament

Letter of James, which asks, "What is your life? For you are like a mist that appears for a little while and then vanishes" (James 4:14). Thus, he encourages each Christian to acknowledge the sober reality of death. This can serve as a bracing and even creative awareness. Knowing that we must die can make us grateful for the days of life we have now. Indeed, a major contemporary American novelist, Tom Wolfe, recounted in an interview that he had suffered a nearly fatal heart attack. After bypass surgery, he figured that if he could live to be eighty-five, he would have a specific number of days to live between his present age and his death. That calculation, he said, made him intensely thankful for and aware of the fullness of each day he now could live.

But death is not only a limit that can teach us to live each day more fully. It is also a mystery that brings a darker side of human existence to the fore. The New Testament, Christian theology, and Christian spirituality have always seen a mysterious link between human sinfulness and death. St. Paul speaks, for example, of sin as "the sting of death" (1 Corinthians 15:56). Paul's meaning may be that sin is separation from God, and that the reality of death, therefore, threatens to make that separation from the source and goal of our lives total and eternal. The sting of death, then, is the dread of eternal separation from God.

If Paul is right, it is natural that severe illness and the thought of death, whether imminent or in the future, should lead people to think seriously about their important relations, especially their relation with God. The Christian tradition has always seen life-threatening illness and the approach of death as an appropriate time for addressing our faithfulness to God. Thus, the Great Litany contains the petition that we not meet death unexpectedly and unprepared (BCP, 149). Jeremy Taylor gives considerable attention to the relation between illness, death, and repentance in *Holy Dying*. When we are ill, especially when seriously ill, he says, we are forced to recognize that we are mortal. This in turn spurs us to respond to the immortal and infinite God whom we will meet in judgment and in grace. As we do so in the Anglican tradition, we are aware of our separation from God and our need for repentance. Because of this, many of the prayers in the Office, "Ministration to the Sick," refer to sin and repentance. We find in the anointing of the sick with oil, for example, that the accompanying prayer reads, "May [God] forgive you your sins, release you from suffering, and restore you to wholeness and strength" (BCP, 456).

An awareness of death not only prompts us to examine our own sinfulness but also forces us to confront the truth that there are tragic deaths and suffering in the world. Theologians term this the "problem of evil." Some deaths are more untimely than others; some seem inexplicable and call into question the justice and love of God. When a child or a person in the prime of life dies, we find ourselves asking: how could a good God grant life to a young person, only to let it end in illness or accident? Tragic death, abruptly bringing a life to its end, brackets and highlights the whole of that life and opens the question of its meaning. Indeed, our realization that everything that has breath will die leads us to ponder the purpose of existence for any living being. Although we resist the idea that death is a punishment for individual sin, we must honestly recognize that the world in which we live, while essentially good, is also a world of death and suffering.

Such darker facets of human life and death lead us to question life's purpose. Ultimately, they may bring many of us to a strengthened faith in a God who is present with us now and forever. Christian faith, in affirming that our existence is meaningful, exposes the powerlessness of death before God's self-expending love. *The Book of Common Prayer* declares: "The liturgy for the dead is an Easter liturgy. It finds all its meaning in the resurrection. Because Jesus was raised from the dead, we, too, shall be raised" (BCP, 507). Moreover, we also recognize that death, even when premature and unwelcome, can bring relief from suffering for a person. And so, as sad as the death of someone we love who is infirm and experiencing suffering can be, it can also be an occasion to thank God for taking that person into God's loving arms, rendering that person "alive . . . with Christ" (Ephesians 2:5). Even as such a death creates in us sorrow, relief, and thankfulness, it heightens our understanding that death opens the door to new life with God in community with others. Thus, an awareness of life's fleeting nature and of the sometimes tragic intrusions of death can often be the starting point of a life of faithful living, a life filled with meaning and purpose that ends in faithful dying.

DEATH AS A SPECIFIC EVENT IN OUR LIVES

Death not only brackets and informs our whole life, but becomes a present and inescapable reality at some crucial point for all of us. It moves into the center of our lives when we learn that we are terminally ill or chronically ill with a condition that will advance inexorably to the event of death. Knowing that we will die impels us to accept that our remaining days are numbered. These days can be, as Jeremy Taylor reminds us in *Holy Dying,* ones of dread or else of eager expectation—or perhaps both intermingled. And, as he and modern writers have observed, they can be days in which we suppress and avoid the truth of the approach of the event of death or ones in which we accept and embrace that truth.

The way in which many of us today experience the event of death has been drastically changed by advances in medicine and changes in our social structure. Most of us will die within a healthcare institution, be it a hospital or nursing home. As these institutions have become more bureaucratized, specialized, and routinized—despite the efforts of many caring professionals and patient representatives—so, too, has death. Death for all too many of us is experienced within a cold, technical environment to which family and friends find it difficult to gain access. The flight of our culture from an acceptance of the reality of death has led it, by neglect, to allow many near death to experience death's arrival within a sterile environment, separated from all held dear. And this isolation and abandonment, even more than any physical pain that we may undergo, is what many of us fear most about death.

The Christian faith calls us to tear away the veil of isolation, estrangement, and medical mechanization with which we have covered the event of death. *The Book of Common Prayer* sees death as a community event, rather than an individual incident in our biological trajectory. The Anglican tradition maintains that we are social at root and that the Christian faith is a corporate faith. It calls us, as Christian members of the human community, to nurture and care for those who are approaching death. It directs us to expose the flimsiness of our culture's attempts to conceal the process of dying and to acknowledge that, while death can still terrify us, it can no longer make good on its threats. It bids us to recognize that the center of our understanding of the event of death and the source of our attitudes of trust, hope, and love, in spite of it, is our faith in the resurrection of the dead. We live in the belief that death is not the final event of our biographies. We know that death opens the way to a transfigured life with others in God.

The Bible offers vivid images and metaphors that point to the richness of our understanding of death and resurrection. We read of the final judgment, of God's mansion with many rooms, of sharing eternal life with the saints, of the redemption of our transformed bodies, of being alive together in Christ, and of a new heaven and a new earth. Death, while still retaining its dreadful and enigmatic quality, becomes, through faith, a doorway into the eternal life of God. By Christ's free acceptance of death in obedience to the Father and for our sake, God has broken its power over our lives. The Christian church therefore teaches us to enter death in Christ—that is, to look upon our death as a journey with Christ through death into the life of God. This is why the final note of Christian faith at the time of death is joy. The Prayer Book Rite, "The Burial of the Dead," intertwines the theme of sadness and loss with the stronger theme of joy and thanksgiving, when it prays at the Eucharist:

> Grant that this Sacrament may be to us a comfort in affliction, and a pledge of our inheritance in that kingdom where there is no death, neither sorrow nor crying, but the fullness of joy with all your saints; through Jesus Christ our Savior. *Amen.* (BCP, 498)

Thus, Christians do not view death as an enemy, capable of destroying all meaning or purpose in our living and in our dying. Rather, we believe that death is a fearful event that God has taken into his own life through Christ and overcome in him. Christian faith enables us to look upon our own dying, and that of people we love, as a journey with Christ through death into the life of God.

This same Christian faith empowers us to acknowledge death in all its terror and destruction. Our journey through death can be accompanied by grief, anxiety, fear, and pain. These are natural responses to death. William F. May points this out:

> The fact of the resurrection of Christ, however, does not mean that the Christian is altogether removed from the experience of natural grief and sorrow. Were it otherwise, the Christian should be able to face his own death without a tremor, and he should be able to walk confidently into the sickroom, contending with its silence by "talking up" a victory that has not yet apparently reached the ears of those who await an imminent defeat. . . . The Christian knows grief in this life. He is not granted on this side of the grave a pure, steadfast, confident, and transparent sense of his limits—or the limits of his neighbor—before God. He tastes of eternal life in Christ, but not a life that removes him from death and the sting of death.[4]

Christian faith does not repress such responses. Instead, because Christians are sustained by the sense of the presence of God in death and dying, we are able to acknowledge our anxieties and losses without being totally overwhelmed by them. The fear, pain, and suffering that we experience as suffusing death can be eased and overcome if we prepare for death spiritually, medically, and morally.

Within the healthcare context, we can do so by using the art and technology of medicine wisely and prudently to serve human purposes. Our call as Christians to live and die faithfully bids us to respond to such questions as how to prepare advance directives to guide medical treatment near the end of life and how to let others know of them. When we have a critical illness that might lead to death, it asks us to assess whether the use of life-sustaining medical technology would be appropriate or whether it would be futile or too burdensome for us and for those we love. It urges us to respond to the question of to what extent we should take charge of our own dying and death. Should we elect to receive palliative care and pain relief as we allow our lives to come to a close or would it, in some circumstances, be morally acceptable for us to end our lives more directly through assisted suicide or euthanasia?[5] The End of Life Task Force discusses these immensely difficult questions and decisions, which have become major social issues in contemporary life, in later chapters of this book. It does so in light of the conviction elaborated here that we should not shield one another from death but should accept and prepare for it, remembering that death has no final power over us.

We have explored the Christian vision of death in this chapter, emphasizing a twofold Anglican understanding of it as a part of our lives and as the final event of our earthly journey. Because we each know we must die, death in a sense is always a part of our lives, even when we are healthy. Yet we have also noted that our contemporary secular culture has been driven to deny the reality of death in a multitude of ways. Christians, in contrast, see death set within a larger story. The key to that story centers in Jesus Christ. Jesus' death and resurrection are fundamental to Christian hope and to the mysterious mixture of sorrow and joy that mark Christian ministry.

Just as a Christian perspective on death can inform faithful living, so, too, can it ease the actual event of our dying. It can help us to prepare for faithful dying and to care for those who are already in the process of dying. Moreover, it can lead us to understand and accept the deaths of those we love dearly. In the following chapter, the End of Life Task Force will pursue the distinctively Anglican understanding of Christian faith as a way of life centered on God, in light of the Christian perspective on the meaning of death and dying set out here.

---

1. David Heinz, *The Last Passage: Recovering a Death of Our Own* (New York: Oxford University Press, 1999).

2. For example, Jessica Mitford, *The American Way of Death* (New York: Simon & Schuster, 1963); *The American Way of Death Revisited* (New York: Alfred A. Knopf, 1998).

3. Jeremy Taylor, *Holy Living and Holy Dying*, 2 vols., ed. P.G. Stanwood (London: Clarendon, 1989). Taylor's original books were respectively published under the titles *The Rule and Exercise of Holy Living* and *The Rule and Exercise of Holy Dying*. This critical edition of these two works combines in the title the often used shortened titles, *Holy Living* and *Holy Dying*.

4. William F. May, "The Sacral Power of Death in Contemporary Experience," in *On Moral Medicine: Theological Perspectives in Medical Ethics*, 2nd ed., ed. Stephen E. Lammers and Allen Verhey (Grand Rapids, Mich.: Eerdmans, 1998), 197–209, 204.

5 See below, Chapter 4, and also "Report of the Task Force on Assisted Suicide to the 122nd Convention of the Episcopal Diocese of Newark," January, 1996; Committee on Medical Ethics, Diocese of Washington, *Assisted Suicide and Euthanasia: Christian Moral Perspectives*, "*The Washington Report*," (Harrisburg, Pa.: Morehouse, 1997); Committee on Medical Ethics, Diocese of Washington, *Toward a Good Christian Death: Crucial Treatment Choices* (Harrisburg, Pa.: Morehouse, 1999).

CHAPTER 2

GOD, DEATH, AND ANGLICAN THEOLOGY

To understand what we mean by faithful living and faithful dying is to understand how the story of Christian faith makes sense of our life in the world. It is to describe the form and central features of a life that Christians share in common, a life that is shaped in distinctive ways by the Anglican tradition. It is to offer an understanding of Christian faith as a way of life that seeks to deepen our relationship with God and that calls us to participate in the purposes of God. And it is to set forth an account of how this way of life shapes our understandings of death and dying.

As Christians, we share the faith that God is present in all of our living, from birth to death, and in our dying. Critical points in our life cycle offer opportunities to experience God more fully, to deepen our relationship with God. Times of new beginnings and losses and of failures and forgiveness are times of crisis for us. They are times of discontinuity, turning points in our lives. At these critical points, the presence of God may be revealed to us, often unexpectedly. This leads us to respond in new ways. We are changed. We experience a shift in our behavior and a shift in our understandings of the world, others, ourselves, and God. Dying and death are among these critical turning points. As we enter into dying, we may gain a new understanding of God's presence and what God is calling us to do and to be.

This new understanding is framed by the central conviction of Christian faith, our belief in one God who is creator and redeemer of the world. To hold this conviction is to claim that there is a power and purpose that gives life. It is to understand that this power that creates and ultimately concludes life is good. It is to believe that what is created by God is also redeemed by God. This faith is expressed in our understanding of life as a gift. The metaphor of gift conveys that life is good and that life, like a gift, is not self-created or self-sufficient. Nothing exists by itself. All of creation is interdependent—the earth, the sky, and all that live therein. An acknowledgment of this gift of life evokes thanks and care from us.

Death reveals the limits of our lives and forcefully reminds us that we are not self-sufficient and self-sustaining. Our aversion to death and our denial of it also expose the extent to which we have turned from the divine life to idolatry. When we identify what is ultimately good with particular, limited, and perishable goods, such as family, culture, work, religion, or pleasures, we create idols. Moreover, to the extent that we substitute these particular goods for our ultimate good, we fear death. Death signals to us the end of these goods. It makes it clear that however marvelous these treasures of life may be, they will not endure forever. When they pass out of existence—as surely all things do—we, too, will die. Consequently, we hang on to these particular goods, clinging to them desperately, afraid to let them go. We live in dread of losing what has been good. Our lives turn narrowly in upon ourselves.

As reflected in the Christian understanding of deadly sins in the Middle Ages, the sin that most threatens the faith of men and women as they approach death is avarice. They covet. They seek to possess, to own and keep forever, the goods of life. Their lives, therefore, become narrowly focused on what they love, so much so that they live only for the sake of preserving what they love. However, they cannot enjoy what is beyond themselves because they cannot love anything for its own sake.

The problem of our lives, Christianity makes clear, is this turning in upon ourselves. As understood by the early Christian theologian, Augustine,[1] our sinfulness is best understood as a matter of idolatry. We misplace our love. Instead of loving the gifts of life as gifts, we come to love them as ends in themselves. We seek to secure them forever. Because death serves notice that nothing is forever, we deny its reality and try to assert our own omnipotence. And when the reality of death surrounds us—which it inevitably does—and we can no longer ignore it, we fall into despair and bitterness. Again, as Augustine explains, as our love becomes constricted in sin, we distort our relationship with God and the world. Our souls fall into bondage, as if slaves to another power. When we are separated from grace, our redemption can come only from the outside. Only grace as a revelation of God frees us from bondage, renews our love, and transforms our lives.

Paradoxically, we die when we deny death. We live when we die to ourselves and live in Christ. As Paul proclaims in his Letter to the Romans, when we are buried and die with Christ, we are raised from the dead that we "might walk in newness of life" (6:4). "If we have died with Christ, we believe that we will also live with him" (6:8). To the outsider to Christian faith, such language of death and resurrection is confusing. What can be meant by life that is given in death? What is the death that is no death? Christians, however, see life and death from another angle. Death is not narrowly a matter of the body but also a matter of the soul. Death is eternal separation from God. Life is life lived in the presence of God. Christian faith is then the trust and hope in this life in God as given in a love that reaches beyond death (1 Corinthians 12:13).

Redemption is therefore a change of heart, a renewed love, an expansion of the human soul or spirit that draws us back into relationship with God. Redemption is not something separate from creation, but is a right ordering of creation. In this sense, faith for Christians is the knowledge of God marked by what are called the theological virtues: faith, hope, and love. Faith is a matter of mind and heart. Knowing God, Christians trust in God and so give themselves to God in hope. At the heart of this faith is the experience of God as a matter of love. As Paul confesses, "neither death, nor life, nor angels, nor rulers, nor things present, nor things to come, nor powers, nor height, nor depth, nor anything else in all creation, will be able to separate us from the love of God" (Romans 8:38–39).

SACRAMENTAL AND EVANGELICAL

In Christian faith there is no final separation between beliefs and actions. We know God, the power that redeems life, only in the living of our lives. This life is grounded in Scripture as celebrated in worship. This is what we mean when we say that Christian faith is given in Word and sacrament. The rich Anglican liturgical tradition of worship expresses this faith as a way of life.[2] Grounded in Word and sacraments, this way of life is evangelical, theocentric, incarnational, and corporate.

For Anglicans, as for other Christians, Scripture is the Word of God in the sense that it is the means by which the voice of God is given and heard. This saving Word is proclaimed in worship as God is recalled, revealed, and known in the offering of our lives in prayer. We consider such worship to be sacramental because it draws us more deeply into relationship with God, enacting the fundamental shape of Jesus' own life as it was given in thanksgiving and love. Nowhere is this worship more fully expressed for Anglicans than in baptism and Jesus' Last Supper. As celebrated in worship, baptism and the Eucharist effect the movement from thanksgiving to offering and sacrifice, from cross to resurrection. They bring a person into faith as a way of life, into what has been called holy living.

This understanding of Christian faith as a way of life has its roots in the early church and the early church fathers. These roots were planted in Benedictine soil and then shaped by the English Reformation. Beginning in the fourth century, monastic communities were established in England.[3] Following the Rule of Benedict, these Benedictine communities were shaped by the disciplines of prayer, study, and work. Worship began, ended, and punctuated each day, as members of the community gathered to read Scripture, sing the Psalms, and offer common prayer of praise and thanksgiving, petition and intercession. The life of prayer was not something separate from daily life but was a celebration and offering of all of life in God. Central to this worship, as part of the seven daily offices of worship, was the reading of Scripture as a *lectio divina,* literally a set of divine readings. These ordered readings provided for meditation on Scripture so that the presence of God could be more deeply known in daily life. Finally, work was not understood as a burden that detracted from faith but was itself a form of prayer, an action of thanksgiving and offering of daily life to God.

Christian faith was for the Benedictines a way of life. Today we speak of their sense of faith, not as a narrow set of religious practices but as forming a life together in God. No doubt monastic communities have drawn away from the world, but their larger vision of a way of life remains central to Anglicanism, especially as it has been shaped by the Reformation in England.

The Reformation brought into being Protestantism, whose central focus is on the open Bible written in the vernacular. As was the case for Benedictines, life in God, for Protestants, is given and deepened through the reading of Scripture. Scripture is the Word of God where God is revealed and known in a way that shapes and transforms our lives. This means that the Bible must be open to all people, hence, translated and read in the language of the people. Worship, in turn, for Protestants, is common worship, a regular gathering of people to listen and hear Scripture. In response, people give thanks and praise for God's grace and offer all of life to God, praying that God's will and not our own may be done. As with the Benedictine communities, religion is not separate from daily life but is the consecration of all of life in God. Religious faith is a matter of holiness, of faithful living in the presence of God.

Influenced by these two sources, Roman Catholic Benedictine communities and Protestant reformers, Anglicanism is a distinctive tradition of Christian faith grounded in Scripture and worship, that is, in Word and sacrament. *The Book of Common Prayer* is at the center of this understanding. Ever since it was given its initial shape by Thomas Cranmer during the English Reformation, the Prayer Book has structured worship around daily offices. Instead of seven offices, Cranmer focused daily worship around two offices, Morning and Evening Prayer. In them, Scripture was read according to a lectionary so that the Old Testament was in large measure read once a year, the New Testament read every four months, and the Psalms read every month.[4] In this way Scripture and prayer shaped the common life of the English people.

The Anglican tradition was able to sustain its understanding of Christian faith as a way of life, at least in part, because it was not caught in the polemical battles that shaped Roman Catholicism and Protestantism during the Reformation, as each fought for dominance in the newly formed nation states in Europe. In separating from Rome and rejecting the formation of a Protestant state, Anglicanism avoided the sharp self-definition of both, at least in terms of theological beliefs. In England, Catholic and Protestant understandings had deeply divided the nation. Requiring all citizens to give allegiance to creedal confessions of faith—whether the Lutheran Augsburg Confession, the Presbyterian Westminster Confession, or those required by the Roman Catholic Church—led only to dissent and punishment, and from there to expatriation or civil war. Under Queen Elizabeth in the sixteenth century, England sought another way. It developed a distinctive Christian tradition in which what is essential to Christian faith is found in common worship and faithful living.

Common worship and faithful living have traditionally been called piety. The word *pious* now is often used to describe someone who is religiously devout in a way that is narrow and somewhat judgmental. However, in its original meaning, piety described a way of life. The *Oxford English Dictionary* defines *piety* simply as the character of a person who is faithful in his or her duties.[5] Jeremy Taylor expressed this understanding of piety in his 1650 classic, *The Rule and Exercise of Holy Living,* an earlier book to which *Holy Dying* is a companion. There he described Christian faith as a matter of piety encompassing duties that are personal, social, and religious—what he speaks of as sobriety, justice, and religion. Christian faith then is for Taylor a way of life, a practical piety, formed in order to "stand before God, acting and speaking, and thinking in His presence."[6]

As is piety, Christian faith is centered in the worship of God, as acknowledgment, praise, and thanks for all that is, and as the offering of life to God in prayer. Again, worship is sacramental in celebrating a way of life that is itself centered in Scripture. This understanding of Christian faith was given its first full expression by Richard Hooker in *The Lawes of Ecclesiastical Politie,* written in the last years of the sixteenth century.[7]

For Hooker, worship stands at the center of life in God as the primary means by which the story of God is heard and known. Scripture, he explained, is saving knowledge of God because it reveals and brings about participation in God's purposes. In worship this scriptural knowledge is effected. Christians participate in the divine life in worship most fully as they reenact in the Holy Eucharist Jesus' offering of himself to God. The Eucharist does not narrowly teach the mind, Hooker declared. Rather, it is a "heavenly ceremony" by which we participate in the divine life. The important thing about the Eucharist is not what we believe happens but that there is "real participation of Christ and of life in his body and blood." Therefore, says Hooker, all should "give themselves to meditate with silence what we have by the sacrament, and less to dispute of the manner how."[8]

This sacramental understanding of Christian faith can be understood too narrowly when worship becomes an end in itself, as if standing in the presence of God were confined to worship apart from daily life. Instead, worship is sacramental in the sense of revealing, celebrating, and effecting the sense of God's presence in all of life. As nineteenth-century Anglican theologian F. D. Maurice said,

> No doubt the world is full of sacraments. Morning and evening, the kind looks and parting words of friends, the laughter of childhood, daily bread, sickness and death; all have a holy and sacramental meaning . . . but then . . . we [need to] have them translated to us.[9]

And this is what the Eucharist does as Christians are joined with Christ in offering to God "our selves, our souls and bodies, to be a reasonable, holy, and living sacrifice unto thee" (BCP, 336). True worship is an eschatological feast, a celebration of the first fruits of faith that are lived out in daily life, in our living and in our dying.

Grounded in Scripture as the story of God, worship is an invitation to enter into relationship with God. In this sense, Christian faith is evangelical, literally *gospel,* good news. Word and sacrament offer saving knowledge that enables a new life and a new understanding of death. Christian faith is a gift from God by which we are changed and so come to participate anew or more fully in the divine life. This means that Scripture and worship must be understood by those who participate in them. For this reason, the Bible and Prayer Book are translated and written in the language of the communities of worship. The Prayer Book is in this sense quite literally *The Book of Common Prayer.*

Within this sacramental and evangelical understanding of Christian faith, Anglicans see death as an occasion in which our relationship to God may be deepened. In fact, death is a privileged occasion, as we have observed earlier, because it raises the question of the meaning and value of life. For this reason, Christians have considered meditation on their own death and on the death of Christ as central spiritual disciplines or exercises. In celebrating Jesus' death and Resurrection in the Eucharist, Christians acknowledge their own deaths and are drawn into faithful dying which, as Jeremy Taylor said, is then to be drawn into faithful living.

THEOCENTRIC, INCARNATE, AND CORPORATE

Grounded in Scripture, Anglican understandings of Christian faith as sacramental and evangelical may be described in terms of three defining features. As a way of life, Christian faith is *theocentric, incarnational,* and *corporate.* It is *theocentric* in its understanding of the purposes of God. That is to say, the completion, reconciliation, and redemption of life is not centered upon some particular aspect of creation or upon individual persons, as if God's purpose were to ensure that some of the many goods of life were to be ultimately realized without end. Instead, the theocentric understanding is that God is one, the beginning and the end, the Alpha and Omega, the creator and redeemer. But to proclaim that God is redeemer is not to understand God as the guarantor of the well being or happiness of any particular being, including humankind. Rather, it is to understand that life is redeemed in God.

The classical Anglican thinker mentioned above, Richard Hooker, articulates this strong theocentric vision in his understanding of God as "law." In ancient philosophy, law meant the end or purpose of something. As such, law may be spoken of as that which orders life as well as the order itself that expresses and gives meaning to life. In this sense God is law, the orderer and the order of things. To use more personal images, God is creator and governor. Hooker's understanding of God in terms of law is misunderstood when law is taken as a set of commands or duties. For Hooker, God is not an arbitrary commander or lawgiver. Instead, God is the power and purpose by which all things move and have their being.

The misunderstanding of God as arbitrary arises because the order of life sometimes seems to cut against the human sense of what would give happiness and fulfillment. It arises when we see the good only in terms of a self-realization of the individual. Instead, as Christian faith is theocentric, centered on God, all that is good is good only in relation to God. Hooker expresses this understanding of the good in his understanding of angels. They offer evidence that God is the center of being, for they seek nothing but God. "Rapt with the love of [God's] beauty, they cleave inseparably for ever unto him."[10] Humans, who are a little lower than the angels, in turn, are to love God like the angels, not for their own well being, but simply because of the goodness of God expressed in the beauty and glory of creation.

Hooker's understanding of God as law—as the power and purpose by which and for which all things are made—ensures that his theocentric vision does not become abstracted from the world. Instead, his understanding of God is also *incarnational*. We know God in and through God's working in the world, as we are acted upon and as we participate in creation. Anglican divines—whether theologians, monks, mystics, poets, or priests—have understood that our knowledge of God is literally enfleshed, given in our bodily experience. The grace of God enfolds us within the world as we are drawn outside ourselves into the glory of God. Thus, faith is the way we live our lives.

This incarnational nature of Christian faith is most fully revealed in Jesus Christ. Because we are fallen from God's grace, we fail to participate fully in the divine life. Our relationship with God is broken. We therefore need a revelation of God that will restore us to that relationship. For

26 FAITHFUL LIVING, FAITHFUL DYING

Anglicans, this restoration is brought about through Word and sacrament. These draw us into the life of God as that is revealed through Jesus Christ—in his teaching and ministry, culminating in his suffering and death on the cross. In this living and dying, Jesus is one with God, raised into God. So, too, in the embrace of God and the love of neighbor, we are drawn out of ourselves into the glory of God. We share in God's kingdom and are raised into eternal life. In this way the presence of God is revealed as incarnate, enfleshed in our living and our dying.

Twentieth-century Anglican theologian and Archbishop of Canterbury William Temple expressed this incarnational understanding by saying that Christianity is the most materialistic religion of the world.[11] The world is affirmed as the creation and gift of God. It is good. It is where we enter into relationship with God. At the same time, Temple emphasized, the incarnation is not to be mistakenly understood as some form of crude materialism. God, as the ultimate good, is not to be confused with some particular aspect of the world that will ultimately pass away. When it is, death is the last word and the cause of despair. Instead, the incarnation means that the goodness of life is not some particular state of affairs but is present throughout life even in the midst of death and dying. God is not "spirit" wholly apart from the world but is enfleshed, incarnate, in the world.

As a third feature, Anglicans have understood Christian faith as *corporate*. Redemption is not individualistic. Creation is itself redeemed as the individual parts and beings are brought into right relationship. In this sense, creation is a community that may be viewed as a holy communion. Christian faith is what brings us back into right relationship with creation. Through Word and sacrament, we are reconciled with God, made one body, the body of Christ, the first fruit of the new creation. This vision of reconciliation and redemption is corporate in the sense that we are incorporated. As the word *incorporated* literally means, we are drawn into one body.

F. D. Maurice expressed the corporate nature of Christian faith in saying that we are created for fellowship, to be in relationship.[12] This, he declared, is the most basic, observable fact of existence. That fellowship or community, which Maurice called "the kingdom of Christ," is simply given. Our call is to live into that kingdom, which knows no bounds. This is the work of creation, now revealed and realized in the body of Christ. Again, faith is to be restored in relationship to God, to be freed from the bondage of sin, to be redeemed and reconciled. This is God's work of love.

As theocentric, incarnate, and corporate, Christian faith does not invariably resolve life's dilemmas. Christians do not have sure and certain answers to the myriad questions and concerns that arise near the end of life. We must grapple long and hard with such matters as whether to begin, continue, or discontinue life-sustaining medical treatment at certain times. This is not to say that all questions about end-of-life care amount to insoluble dilemmas or that Christian faith offers us no guidance when we are perplexed about them. Rather, most importantly, our faith shapes our basic understandings of and attitudes toward life and death. It forms us such that we are sensitive and responsive to God in matters of life and death. Our Christian understandings and attitudes increase our awareness of what ought to be valued in our living and in our dying. They also shape and enable the response of those who are dying and of many who are related to the dying—family, friends, and neighbors.

Christian faith is not like an accurate observation, as in answering whether or not the sun is shining. Instead, faith is a conviction about the nature of things that is itself grounded in distinct experiences. When Christians say, "I am struck by grace," we mean that we are so convicted that we understand, even in the midst of doubt, that the world is the loving creation of God. Such an understanding is a matter of the heart as well. To understand the world as the loving creation of God is to have an attitude of trust, hope, and love, the three theological virtues. It is to enter the critical turning points of dying and death trusting that God is present in them as in all of life.

We now turn to consider how our grasp of the Christian way of life is further expanded by the ethical understandings and moral meanings that are distinctive to our tradition. These theological and ethical understandings together will serve to shed light on the sensitive and often agonizing questions that arise for many of us today who are near the end of life.

---

1. See, for example, Augustine, "The Nature of the Good," *Augustine: Earlier Writings,* J. H. S. Burleigh, ed. (Philadelphia: Westminster Press, 1953), 325–348.

2. For an account of Anglicanism, including discussions of Anglican divines, see Stephen Sykes and John Booty, eds., *The Study of Anglicanism* (London and Philadelphia: SPCK/ Fortress, 1988). The account given here draws especially from Timothy F. Sedgwick, *The Christian Moral Life* (Grand Rapids, Mich.: Eerdmans/Forward Movement, 1999), 25–51. See also Paul Elmen, "Anglican Morality," in Sykes and Booty; David H. Smith, *Health and Medicine in the Anglican Tradition* (Crossroad, 1986), 5–44; and Alan M. Suggate, "The Anglican Tradition of Moral Theology," *Worship and Ethics,* Oswald Bayer and Alan Suggate, eds. (Berlin and New York: Walter de Gruyter, 1996), 2–25.

3. See Bede, *A History of the English Church and People,* tr. Leo Sherley Price (Baltimore: Penguin, 1955); written by the monk Bede in 731, this offers a firsthand account of the beginnings of Christianity in England.

4. For a history of *The Book of Common Prayer* see Marion J. Hatchett, "Prayer Books," *The Study of Anglicanism,* Stephen Sykes and John Booty, eds. (London and Philadelphia: SPCK/Fortress, 1988), 121–133.

5. *Oxford English Dictionary,* 2nd ed. (Oxford: Oxford University Press, 1991), vol. 11, 804.

6. Jeremy Taylor, *Holy Living and Holy Dying,* 2 vols., ed. P. G. Stanwood (London: Clarendon, 1989), vol. 1, 24. As noted earlier, Taylor's original books were respectively published under the titles *The Rule and Exercise of Holy Living* and *The Rule and Exercise of Holy*

Dying. This critical edition of these two works combines in the title the often used shortened titles, *Holy Living and Holy Dying.*

7. Richard Hooker, *The Lawes of Ecclesiastical Politie,* 7 vols., Folger Library Edition, Speed Hill, ed. (Cambridge, Mass.: Harvard University Press, 1977–1981).

8. *The Lawes of Ecclesiastical Politie,* V.67.3.

9. F. D. Maurice, *The Kingdom of Christ,* ed. Alec Vidler (London: SCM, 1958), vol. 2, 81.

10. *The Lawes of Ecclesiastical Politie,* I.4.1

11. William Temple, *Nature, Man, and God* (London: Macmillian, 1934), 478.

12. F. D. Maurice, *The Kingdom of Christ,* vol. 1, 228.

CHAPTER 3

MORAL JOURNEY, ETHICAL COMPASS

Facing our own frailty and mortality, making choices about medical care near the end of life, and caring for others for whom death approaches—these are all-too-human endeavors that call upon most of us to reach out to something beyond this life, to something transcendent. As we grapple with these human matters, we look for meaning, guidance, and a sense of purpose. What has my life meant? Have I traveled the right path? What lies beyond?

As the previous chapter indicated, we attempt, as Christians, to comprehend the situation at the end of life from a God-centered or theocentric perspective. This theological approach suggests a distinctive perspective on ethics as well. None of the experiences of human life, including those near death, should be separated from the quest to understand God and God's purposes for humankind in creation. The faith that there is a divine purpose for humanity and that we are called to a life-long journey in which we are to live out this truth are the twin pillars of a Christian conception of ethics and the moral life. Thus, we approach the ethical dimension of end-of-life care and decision making mindful of the overarching reality of God's grace and redemptive love.

As Christians, we share in many of the conclusions offered by contemporary moral philosophy, the tradition of medical ethics, and the law concerning ethical issues related to end-of-life care. The Episcopal Church has addressed some of these matters through General Convention resolutions[1] and diocesan publications[2] and will continue to do so over time. What is important in this chapter, however, is not so much the specific conclusions and recommendations the Church has come to in the past or those that we shall offer later in this book. What is important here is the route of reflection and discernment used to reach these conclusions. The question at this point is not *what* Christians should think about ethics at the end of life, but *how* they think about ethics at the end of life, and at other times as well. The End of Life Task Force aims to convey the spirit of that reflection, clarify its assumptions, and trace its roots in light of the Anglican understanding of Christian faith as a way of life.

With a style, voice, and spirit drawn from the Anglican tradition, the task force offers a distinctive Christian vision of what ethical discernment near the end of life involves. One major difference in our approach from that of secular medical ethics is that we do not perceive ethical reflection to be the product of human reason alone but also a response to God.[3] Ethical understanding takes place within the context of our daily life-orientation toward God. Ethics is like a compass for navigating the moral life: it helps us find our way, and it gives us a sense of direction. But without a magnetic north to orient and impel it, the compass needle would spin and be useless to us. God is our Magnetic North.

Moreover, in the Anglican tradition, ethical understanding is not seen as the creation of an isolated, skeptical mind seeking to sweep away the past and build ethical conclusions upwards from a few bedrock principles. This image of the lone mind and this deductivist conception of practical reasoning are not the starting points for Christian ethics in the Anglican tradition. Oriented toward God, our starting point is corporate. That is, the moral life is a communal project lived in the presence of—and in relationship to—God and our fellow human beings.[4] Ethics flourishes in the context of a community of mutual respect, shared tradition, reasoned commitment, and freely given service and love.

This Anglican moral vision offers fresh insight into the difficult and poignant questions that arise for those in the advanced stages of illness, those who are clearly dying, and their families. It offers an approach toward God and the community that is urgently needed today as the healthcare system attempts to improve the way it provides palliative and humanely respectful care near the end of life. This vision can offer a lens through which to view individual and family decisions, clinical decisions by physicians and other healthcare professionals, and public policy decisions concerning end-of-life care.

ETHICS AND THE MORAL LIFE

Some contemporary writers use the term *morality* to refer to existing practices, beliefs, and rules that characterize a particular culture, while they take the term *ethics* to refer to the systematic study and principled justification of morality.[5] For them, morality is what is believed to be right, while ethics refers to why it is believed to be right.

There are good reasons, however, to keep morality and ethics from drifting too far apart. For one thing, we do not obey rules mindlessly; we also reflect on the broader meaning and justification of these rules. We are guided by the historical traditions and prevailing systems of morality in our society, as well as by Scripture, reason, and the traditions of the Church. The Anglican emphasis on faith as a way of life leads this tradition to give special weight to the experience of the lived moral life. Ethics and morality, for Anglicans, are intertwined. Because of this, we shall follow common parlance and use *ethics* and *morality* synonymously here to refer to a moral form of life that is both reflective and practically grounded. This, moreover, is in keeping with the etymological origins of the terms. *Ethos* (from the Greek) and *mores* (from the Latin) both refer to proper structures and styles of living together, the fitting forms of human social life.

The moral life is properly seen as living in obedience to a structure of rules or commandments. Yet our moral experience is not exclusively made up of matters of right and wrong that are clearly set forth, nor is our lived moral experience just a series of value quandaries or situations of choice in which we must grasp one of two horns of a dilemma. Instead, living as a moral person also has a more dynamic, searching quality. Thus, much of our moral experience consists of finding our way and taking our bearings in relationship to others, our own conscience, and purposes broader and higher than our own.[6]

A moral education involves learning to read and follow our ethical compass around the space of the moral life. This means not just watching out for the warning signs or rules that others have posted but also leaving the well-marked trails and coming to know the full terrain and texture of the moral life. Just as this is true of moral experience over the whole course of our lives, so too is it true of our moral experience in the face of dying and death.

Something akin to this understanding of the moral life as a journey of discovery is found in the sacrament of baptism, the foundation of our identity as Christians for the Anglican tradition. The symbolism of the individual's rebirth in Christ through water signifies a fundamental setting of life's compass, a reorientation so that the person now faces in the proper direction. The words of the sacrament express the upcoming drama of human life on earth as a struggle not to turn away from this orientation and direction, for "falling into sin" is precisely that turning away.

Moreover, the individual is not alone in this struggle; the entire community is called upon first to recalibrate its own orientation, with each member of the company recalling his or her own baptismal covenant, and then to promise to support the newly baptized person. Part of that support consists in appropriate teaching and instruction. Also implicit in the sacrament is the notion that, in order to be properly oriented toward God, each person must be properly oriented to the other members of that community, and indeed to all humankind. The community itself constitutes an orienting environment for each person.

The sacrament reminds us that the moral life involves interplay among human ability, will, and intention, exercised with the assistance of divine grace. The response in the ethical portion of the covenant places these elements together clearly: "I will, with God's help." Human agency is central within the Anglican moral tradition. Thus, the baptismal covenant begins with a reaffirmation of creedal beliefs and of faith, and then turns to the life of action.

First comes religious practice—the teaching, fellowship, the breaking of bread, and the prayers. Then comes moral life in society. Particular elements of morality are singled out in this covenant, and they have special significance for understanding the shape and priorities of morality.

> Will you persevere in resisting evil, and whenever you fall into sin, repent and return to the Lord? . . . Will you proclaim by word and example the Good News of God in Christ? . . . Will you seek and serve Christ in all persons, loving your neighbor as yourself? . . .Will you strive for justice and peace among all people, and respect the dignity of every human being?[7]

We are on a journey in which we are to persevere, resist, return, seek, strive, love, and respect. The picture that we derive of the moral life as a dramatic journey is reinforced in the prayers. Here we find the rhythms of God's action upon those about to be baptized. God will "deliver," that is, properly orient the person, and then "open" and "fill," "keep" and "teach," "send" and "bring." The properly oriented moral life will be one of openness to others, confidence and efficacy, membership and a sense of belonging, willingness to learn, an urge to go out into the world, and finally a homecoming to the source of our being.

No less instructive is what the sacrament has to say about the types of human relationships that should grow out of the struggle for a moral life lived toward these graceful ends. Here we find, of course, the word and example of God in Christ. Then, singled out for special emphasis we find the social goals of equality, justice, peace, and respect for human dignity, as well as concepts defining the appropriate types of interaction among human beings—service, love, and respect. Here, in a very compressed text and with beautiful economy of expression, we find a remarkable portrait of the moral life.

Ethical reflection is an integral part of the Christian moral life as the sacrament of baptism conceives it. It is the vocation of ethics to raise fundamental questions about how we should live our lives and how we should treat others. In response, ethical reflection and discernment draws upon a rich array of concepts and categories in order to articulate ideals and aspirations, as well as duties and rules.

Let us briefly review some of the elements with which ethical reflection works. Ethics addresses virtues of character, as well as principles of conduct or action. It reflects on the interests and flourishing of the individual, as well as on justice and the good of the community. Because of the diversity of the moral life and the complexity of the human condition, ethical reflection is characterized by sometimes conflicting, sometimes complementary, concepts. It encompasses many values, which we believe ultimately to be unified within the love and will of God. Among them are individual liberty, rights, autonomy, an obligation to respect others, a duty to refrain from harming others, justice, courage, mercy, trust, empathy, community, fidelity, and love.

Such values, obligations, ideals, and virtues provide the framework for the moral life. And it is the moral life within which individuals act, make judgments, develop character and conscience, and, finally, over time and by the grace of God, flourish and grow more fully human.

Moreover, ethics evaluates our conduct in terms of its purposefulness in honoring or realizing moral values—that is, those states of being in the world that are right or good. Broadly speaking, the study of ethics involves a consideration of three aspects of moral conduct: first, the intentions, goals, or purposes with which we act; second, the motives, interests, and beliefs that drive our actions; and third, the consequences of our actions, both in terms of their effects on others and in terms of the values they honor and bring into the world.

This last point is not discussed much in secular ethics and deserves further emphasis. The study of ethics is designed to shed light on the multifaceted ways in which our conduct as humans creates, discloses, or otherwise brings value into the world. Three of these have particular relevance to caring and decision making near the end of life.

Actions express values. Actions are guided by the agent's commitment to values; that is what it means to say that an action is intentional or purposive. Thus, the agent's action has already been evaluated by him or her as suited to some purpose; the action reveals that evaluation, reflecting the agent's intention. An ethical evaluation then involves assessing whether the agent's intention or purpose is ethically sound, given our shared framework of meaning and values.

Actions embody values. Actions can bring values into the world by "embodying" them, by giving form and shape to right and good states of being. Some actions enhance the goodness of the world just by their performance, whether they have any consequences or not. Acts of love, respect, or prayer embody value in this way. An act of faithful witness and presence, such as keeping watch at the bedside over a dying person, embodies value in and of itself, even if no one else is there to see and even if the patient herself is unconscious and unaware at the time. Of course, actions also bring value into the world by having certain effects on the world and on others. Such actions may have no intrinsic value, no particular value in themselves, but are the medium through which something else of value may be realized. Thus, building a fence beside a dangerous road, a valueless activity when done to no purpose or effect, can bring greater safety into the world and perhaps save the life of a child.

Actions enable values. Human action is often the medium through which the goodness and righteousness that God has bestowed upon us are made actual and potent. Thus, in addition to being expressed and embodied by action, values are also "enabled" by actions. What we have in mind are those times when values come alive in relations among persons. Just saying or doing the graceful, fitting, and appropriate thing can kindle courage and resolve, elicit compassion, foster respect, nurture caring and fidelity, or call forth mercy. Many times actions enable moral value through healing, repair, or restoration. The Hebrew phrase *tikkun olam,* which means "to mend the fabric of the world," expresses precisely what we have in mind here.

When we assess actions in light of the ways they enable values, we need to consider long-term as well as short-term effects. How a person acts now may enable or "disable" the capacity of others to realize values in their lives and action, either now or in the future. Some acts may upset the balance of justice and right relations among persons, or they may further human flourishing and help us "do all such good works as [God has] prepared for us to walk in" (BCP, 339).

None of these three varieties of moral evaluation can be ignored or omitted in our understanding of the ethical situation of human earthly life, including its closing chapter. Ethics must consider the intention in action, the motivation behind action, and the effects of action. And ethics must also consider the many ways in which human actions bring value into the world, for these ways are subtle and nuanced. They do not always fulfill the agent's intention or satisfy the motive behind the act, and they are not always direct, immediate, or easy to observe in their effects; nonetheless, they can be real and morally significant.

BROADENING THE PERSPECTIVE OF ETHICS IN END-OF-LIFE CARE

Most secular ethical discussions regarding end-of-life care tend to focus on a model of the relationship between patients and healthcare professionals (and of human social relationships generally) that is based on individual rights and interests. This model depicts human beings as moral atoms who are not naturally in community with one another but who form artificial social ties based on interest and need. The moral life, on this account, primarily consists of making claims, demands, and promises or contracts. Healthcare relationships, in particular, are couched in terms of rights, contractual obligations, and the exchange of goods and services.

This model has been a powerful force in recent years for changing the culture and practice of health care for the better in many ways. It has promoted patient rights and it has reduced the authoritarianism and paternalism that were once accepted in the treatment of patients. Useful as it has been for some purposes, however, this model is often not well suited to addressing the kinds of ethical questions that permeate end-of-life care. The individualistic emphasis on rights and control that is at its base does not adequately capture our human experience of mortality, disease, dependency, grief, hope, and despair at the end of life. Moreover, this individualistic framework, in focusing on a contractually based doctor-patient relationship, tends to remove care giving and decision making from the vital contexts of the family and close friends, the broader community, and the patient's own biographical narrative. Offering no social vision of what a good death could mean, it leaves each individual to puzzle out, on his or her own, how to go about dying. In essence, it turns John Donne's marvelous trope upside down. Donne recalls that:

> No man is an Iland, intire of it selfe; every man is a peece of the Continent, a part of the maine; . . . any mans death diminishes me, because I am involved in Mankinde; And therefore never send to know for whom the bell tolls; It tolls for thee.[8]

In an individualistic framework, however, our mortality is not seen, as Donne would have it, as an equalizing and binding force of shared vulnerability, frailty, and dependency. Individualism does not hear the funeral bell for the entire community. In it, the bell tolls eventually for each of us, to be sure, but it tolls for us one at a time.

The Anglican tradition offers a more communal understanding of who the patient is and of how, near the end of life, moral authority flows from that patient to the family, to those close to him or her, and to the community. The past and present relationship among them is a significant binding force within Anglicanism. Thus, we ask somewhat different questions from those our society has been asking of the sick and debilitated who face death.

What understanding of the nature of the moral life will be helpful for a fuller appreciation of the ethical and spiritual challenges of end-of-life care? And what light can the Anglican tradition shed by dint of its distinctive feel for the ethical dimension of our lives on issues that arise as we approach the end of life?

In light of our understanding of Anglican theology and ethics, outlined in this and the preceding chapter, we conclude our general discussion of ethics and the moral life by suggesting three themes that pervade the more concrete ethical issues that will be discussed in the second part of this book. These are that we ought to use power and technology responsibly, sustain right relationships among persons, and promote the human good both individually and communally.

• *End-of-life care calls for the responsible use of human power.* Terminally ill persons and those with advanced illness leading to death are among the most vulnerable and powerless of persons. All who interact with them, professionals and lay caregivers alike, have a measure of power over them that they are called to exercise responsibly. Moreover, advances in medical science and technology provide physicians with tremendous power that can affect the timing and the quality of the person's dying. In some cases dying can be extended and prolonged considerably, either to the patient's benefit or to that person's grave harm. Therefore, technology and the power inherent in it should be used thoughtfully, respectfully, lovingly, and responsibly.

• *End-of-life care calls for right relationships among persons.* Dying persons are not mere bodies or collections of organ systems in states of dysfunction, although, as we noted in chapter 1, there is much in the culture of medicine today that leads doctors to view patients in that abstract, dehumanizing way. In defining the character of right relationships in the context of care near the end of life, we must inquire whether it is appropriate to carry over the notions we routinely employ for healthy adults in everyday life to those near death. Do the usual notions of independence and individualism apply without modification to the care of the dying? Or might such concepts present obstacles to acknowledging fully the reality that envelops those approaching death? Might they impose a moral blinder obscuring the magnitude of the responsibility that impending death actually poses for health professionals, spiritual counselors, family, and friends? Questions about right relationships, exceedingly difficult as they are, must be explored near the end of life.

• *End-of-life care calls for relationships, resources, and empowerment that promote human good.* Is our journey any the less important because it is nearing its temporal and earthly end? Too often in our culture, those who are dying are thought of as a separate class of persons for whom the notion of promoting human good seems odd or inapplicable. Too often they are cut them off from the rest of the human community. The task force regards this as a fallacy and a mistake. We insist instead on the need to evaluate systems, resources, and practices in end-of-life care from the perspective of how well they serve the patient's dignity, personhood, meaningful identity, and status as a neighbor to be loved as ourselves, even as death approaches. "As you did it to one of the least of these who are members of my family, you did it to me" (Matthew 25:40).

How does the perspective offered here compare with the model of secular individualism described earlier? The main threat that such individualism sees in the circumstances of contemporary medical care at the end of life is that someone may override the autonomous will of the dying person. Attention to the responsible use of human power reveals, however, that in end-of-life care situations the dying person is in danger not simply of being overruled but of being morally eclipsed by the lure of life-sustaining medical technology. There is a kind of idolatry at work in the so-called technological imperative[9] such that the intrinsic dignity of the person is displaced by the assumed intrinsic value of the machine. The social and legal norm protecting the right of the competent patient to refuse medical treatment is appropriate, not only as a means of empowering the choosing individual but also as a means of preserving the very moral identity of that person.

Further, the injunctions given in secular ethical discussions are often negative in character. Above all, do no harm; do not violate the individual's rights; do not take power away from the patient. Such injunctions are ethically essential, but also ethically incomplete. They provide fences, but no common meeting place. They protect rights, but offer only a thin basis for promoting the human good.

In contrast, the Anglican tradition is predicated on the belief that there is a common moral ground available to human beings. This common ground is centered on the call to use human power responsibly, to establish right relationships among us, and to promote human flourishing. Thus, when we attempt to address difficult matters that arise near the end of life, we bring to bear an ethical perspective that, while distinctively Anglican, bears a shared core of meaning that also speaks to a multitude of others with whom we are drawn together in our diverse society. As we turn to Part II, in which we address putting into effect a distinctively Anglican practical piety for those near death, we are mindful of the mutually sustaining relationships we can marshal as a community to attend to the care of these vulnerable and needful persons.

---

1. General Convention resolutions relevant to moral and theological issues that arise near the end of life are brought together in the appendix of Committee on Medical Ethics, Episcopal Diocese of Washington, *Toward a Good Christian Death: Crucial Treatment Choices* (Harrisburg, Pa.: Morehouse, 1999).

2. Committee on Medical Ethics, Episcopal Diocese of Washington, *Before You Need Them: Advance Directives for Health Care, Living Wills and Durable Powers of Attorney* (Cincinnati, Ohio: Forward Movement Publications, 1995); Committee on Medical Ethics, Episcopal Diocese of Washington, *Assisted Suicide and Euthanasia: Christian Moral Perspectives, "The Washington Report"* (Harrisburg, Pa.: Morehouse, 1997); Committee on Medical Ethics, Episcopal Diocese of Washington, *Toward a Good Christian Death: Crucial Treatment Choices,* (Harrisburg, Pa.: Morehouse, 1999).

3. For a thorough discussion of the implications of taking a God-centered orientation in ethics, see James M. Gustafson, *Ethics from a Theocentric Perspective,* 2 vols. (Chicago, Illinois: University of Chicago Press, 1983), vol. 1, 68–113.

4. See David H. Smith, *Health and Medicine in the Anglican Tradition* (New York: Crossroad, 1986), 5–34.

5. For example, in a widely used college ethics textbook, Vincent Barry writes: "The term *ethics* is sometimes used synonymously with morals. It would be more accurate, though, to use the terms *morals* and *moral* to refer to the conduct itself, and terms ethics and ethical to refer to the study of moral conduct or to the code one follows." *Applying Ethics,* 2d ed. (Belmont, Calif.: Wadsworth, 1985), 5. It is interesting to note that in the third edition of this book, the discussion including the above quotation is omitted and no systematic distinction between ethics and morals is made.

6. Compare Dietrich Bonhoeffer, *Ethics* (New York: Macmillan, 1965), 253: "In responsibility both obedience and freedom are realized. Responsibility implies tension between obedience and freedom. There would be no more responsibility if either were made independent of the other. Responsible action is subject to obligation, and yet it is creative."

7. *The Book of Common Prayer,* 304–305.

8. John Donne, *Devotions Upon Emergent Occasions,* Meditation XVII, in Charles M. Coffin, ed., *The Complete Poetry and Selected Prose of John Donne* (New York: Random House, 1952), 441.

9. The technological imperative holds that if something can be done (successfully), then it should be done. This notion has been tenacious in regard to medical treatment near the end of life since so many real medical and scientific advances have been made in recent years.

CHAPTER 4

USING OUR MEDICAL
POWERS APPROPRIATELY

The Anglican moral vision calls upon us to use our medical powers responsibly near the end of life. In our actions at this time, whether they involve pressing ahead with medical treatment or stopping it, we are bidden to embody and express the values that define us as Christians. These values are undergirded by the Anglican understanding of the incarnational nature of Christian faith, which urges us to care for those near death in a way that embodies the presence of God. They are supported by its theocentric understanding of God as creator and redeemer; this leads us to recognize that those near death are our neighbors who are of importance to God. And they are upheld by its corporate emphasis and recognition of our mutual interdependence, calling us to be concerned not only for the good of individuals, but also for the common good. With these values in mind, we turn in Part II to consider how this Anglican moral vision illumines a set of topics that raise pressing questions about appropriate choices and care near the end of life.

Our advanced medical powers, we have observed, give us the ability to keep people alive today much longer than ever before. While this is a cause for rejoicing, it is also a cause for concern. All too often medical technology has the power to keep us alive but is unable to function in ways that allow us to realize our purposes as human beings. It can extend our life but fail to restore us to a condition in which that life is meaningful. Thus, questions abound. Should we acquiesce in the face of death or attempt to use medical technology to remain alive as long as possible? Should we use narcotics to alleviate pain and suffering if they will hasten the point of death? Should we allow death to arrive in due course or bring it about more directly by means of physician-assisted suicide?

These are exceptionally difficult questions that do not lend themselves to simple responses by formula. They require ethical discernment that flows from an understanding of our Anglican call to use human power responsibly, to create right relationships among us, and to promote human good. They call out for a forthright Christian response that is informed by the Anglican way of life.

THE USES AND MISUSES OF MEDICAL TECHNOLOGY IN LIGHT OF THE GOALS OF MEDICINE

Our conviction that God cares for and governs the universe puts our expanding set of tools for extending life into a context of thanksgiving. Moreover, our understanding that we live rightly as finite beings when we live in response to God's presence evokes an attitude of gratefulness in us for these marvelous technological measures. We celebrate them as achievements reached through God's gifts of human intelligence and art, as ways of sustaining ourselves and our community. Anglicanism resists any idea that biomedical science or technology is intrinsically perverse or suspect, that it somehow detracts from God's sovereignty. To the contrary, it views the use of human imagination, reason, and skill to invent and use these technologies in diagnostically appropriate ways as a sacred calling, a form of ministry to humankind.

Yet another implication of these Christian understandings is that it is possible for us to misuse this medical technology. We do so when we sustain life longer than is appropriate or fitting. To be human is to be finite; we are "absolute" or "eternal" only insofar as we share in the presence of God. Thus, Anglicanism rejects as idolatrous a vitalism that contends that persons should live indefinitely or must be kept biologically alive as long as is medically possible. Surely, other things being equal, more life is better than less. Things are not always equal, however, and increasingly decisions about what treatment is most fitting need to be made in humility, love, and hope. Anglicanism rejects any ideology that pretends that making decisions about whether to sustain life by modern medical means can be avoided. We cannot simply assume that we must use a technology because it is available. Instead, we must make a deliberate decision about whether to proceed with its use.

The goals of medicine and human purposes. Assessing when we misuse medical technology requires us to consider what we want to accomplish and this, in turn, leads us to ask about the goals of medical treatment. The primary goal of medicine is not just to treat or ameliorate a particular physical or psychological condition, to cure an injury or illness, to extend human life, or to relieve suffering—although these are important goals. Decisions to treat or not to treat, and then about how to treat, are made for the sake of the human person. Thus, the primary goal of medicine is to promote human health, not in the narrow sense of physical well-being or mental cohesiveness, but in the sense conveyed by the literal meaning of the term *health*—wholeness. The purpose of medicine is to honor and enhance the wholeness of the human person, the health of the person.[1]

The whole person, for Christians, is given in the unity of body and soul. In and through our bodies we know the world about us. We see, touch, hear, feel, and taste. In and through our bodies, we act and make things happen. We create and we intervene; we speak and we embrace. Who we are, what we know, and how we love are given in and through our bodies. We are incarnate beings. In this sense, we say as Christians that our bodies were created for something more than bodily life itself. Health, therefore, is not narrowly focused on the body, but on body and soul, and thus on the ends and purposes of human life. Some of the complex questions that can arise at the end of life challenge us to understand how we can realize these ends and purposes in the midst of dying. These questions center on human suffering, both physical and spiritual. The medical treatment that extends our lives may also cause suffering. And what relieves that suffering may cause suffering of yet another kind.

Pain and suffering are distinct and yet closely interrelated experiences. The experience of pain is of what hurts, as when we speak of a sharp pain or an enduring pain. The experience of suffering is of the limitations pressed upon us because of something beyond us, something beyond our control. Suffering can be as hurtful or even more hurtful than pain. We may suffer from the loss of a friendship more than we suffer from the pain of injuries. In terms of health, we suffer not only from illness and the pain it may engender but also from the limitations imposed upon us by medical treatment. Medical treatments that can no longer cure can assault the ends, purposes, and values of our life. And we can suffer from this.

For example, consider a case where a man has cancer for which radiation treatment and drugs may no longer hold hope for cure; treatments are given to him instead to slow the tumor's growth, to effect a period of remission, to extend his life for a time. However, the man experiences nausea, exhaustion, and depression from the treatment. The regimen disrupts the rhythms and relations that he most values in daily life. Always there is more that could be done to treat him, but he suffers from the limitations that further treatment imposes on him. The "success" in view for this man cannot be defined narrowly in terms of "combating" the progression of his disease, but in terms of what would enhance the whole person. The possible benefits and likely burdens of medical treatment, including the suffering induced by treatment itself, need to be weighed against each other both before medical treatment is undertaken and when it is continued. Moreover, these benefits and burdens need to be viewed broadly in terms of how they express, embody, and affect such values as love, justice, loyalty, and beneficence for this person. At some point, the future benefit of extending this man's life will not be great enough to outweigh the suffering, losses, and limitations it causes him. When this becomes true, his medical treatment must be said no longer to have "a reasonable chance of success." His human good and his human purposes are no longer served by extending his life.

Those who are seriously ill and advancing toward death should be treated in light of their human purposes. Specific judgments by patients about how these purposes can be honored when treatment is at issue will, of course, vary since each person's journey is uniquely his or her own. The man above may willingly undergo the burden of further treatment so that he might live long enough to see the birth of a grandchild. Another person in similar circumstances might forgo treatment—even though this might result in an earlier death—because he can spend time now, and not later, with family and friends. Thus, the end of medical treatment is always health and wholeness in light of human purposes.

The hope for a miracle. As this discussion implies, Anglicanism insists that serious religious faith is not to be isolated from all reasoning and reflective perspectives about medical treatment. Faith infuses reason. The action of God is not an *alternative* to human action and choice, to human responsibility. Rather, God's ongoing action presents us with the possibility and problem of discerning how best to respond. God then acts through our responsive actions. Thus, the question of what form of treatment to use in a specific instance does not all of a sudden receive a religious answer because someone invokes a hope for a miracle. We sometimes hear, in the midst of a discussion of what should be done for a beloved relative, "I know it looks bad, but we should continue treatment and hope for a miracle!" Of course, continuing treatment may well be the fitting thing to do in this instance, but the appeal to a special divine intervention to resolve the question departs from a distinctively Anglican attention to the particularities of the situation. It makes considerations of patient comfort, patient purposes, strain on the family, or treatment expense seem less serious morally and spiritually than Anglicanism believes them to be. Thus, appeals to a possible miraculous intervention by God may preempt us from grappling fully and reasonably with these "mundane" considerations that are, in truth, of importance.

There is a time for turning over our lives and the lives of those we love to God. Recognition of human limits is crucial. This is not to suggest that Anglicanism rejects the possibility of miraculous cures. Obviously, it does not. It is to point out that the miraculous in God's care for us at the end of life is not revealed only in the inexplicable. It is also seen in the power of accurate diagnosis and prescription, in the joyful recognition of family members, and in the reconciliation of the estranged.

WHETHER WE ARE MORALLY REQUIRED TO PROVIDE ARTIFICIAL NUTRITION AND HYDRATION TO THOSE NEAR DEATH

Many forms of life-sustaining treatments can be provided for those who are approaching the end of life. Whether to withhold or withdraw such treatments from them can become an agonizingly difficult question for them and for us as we seek to use our power responsibly and to maintain right relationships with one another. This question arises, for instance, when the use of artificial feeding, including nutrition (for example, through a feeding tube inserted into the stomach) and hydration (most often intravenously, through a tube inserted into a vein), is considered. This is a fairly new question about which the End of Life Task Force thinks it imperative that Anglicans engage in prayerful and thoughtful discussion.

One aspect of this matter that makes it vexing is the need to describe appropriately what is at issue. If we speak of providing "artificial nutrition and hydration," the process seems a creation of modern high-tech medicine. When viewed in these terms, it is morally right to remove such technology from those for whom it is disproportionately burdensome or futile. However, if we refer instead to providing "food and water" or "basic nutrition," the act seems a natural and caring one to perform. We view feeding as a deeply symbolic act of love to which we attach extraordinary meaning. In these terms, it strikes us as morally wrong to discontinue to provide food to vulnerable persons who are dying.

Certainly, depriving the weak of needed food and drink is a paradigmatic case of individual and social sin within the Christian tradition. Even so, we must recognize that having a synthetic protein compound pumped directly into the intestine by skilled medical personnel is not the same as eating and drinking with friends. It is a qualitatively different act from feeding a patient with a cup and a spoon. Therefore, the task force maintains that sustaining a person by artificial nutrition and hydration constitutes a medical intervention.[2] We believe that this view appropriately conveys the nature of artificial feeding. As a form of medical treatment, it may be declined or ended when it is burdensome or futile.

There is a moral presumption that persons who are seriously ill and approaching death should receive some form of feeding—be it artificial or by cup and spoon—to avoid an uncomfortable death. This presumption needs to be set aside, however, when the use of available forms of feeding would be disproportionately burdensome to the patient, contrary to human ends and purposes. To determine when this would be the case, the various forms of feeding available need to be assessed in terms of their effects in themselves and also more broadly in terms of whether each ultimately would promote the human purposes of the person who is dying.

Burdens of artificial nutrition and hydration near the end of life.
Artificial feeding in itself can compromise the ends or purposes of life. It
can create disproportionate burdens, depending on the kind of technical
feeding procedure used. Inserting a stomach tube requires intrusive
surgery; a nasogastric feeding tube can be highly irritating and bother-
some to patients. Furthermore, we learn from hospice physicians and
nurses that if either artificial or regular feeding is imposed on patients near
death who are functionally unable to assimilate it, they experience considerable suffering.[3] To this they add that those who are near death generally
do not experience hunger and do not have a sense of "starvation" or thirst
if they refuse artificial or regular feeding, as long as a dry mouth or other
attendant physical discomfort is alleviated.[4] Moreover, artificial feeding
may make the dying person and those caring for him or her (families,
friends, and caregivers) feel physically separated at a time when human
relationships are especially important. Finally, the costs of such treatment
can present a serious difficulty. The use of artificial feeding, therefore, can
inflict some significant burdens that patients and families have no obligation to suffer. In such instances, there can be a moral need to withdraw
artificial nutrition and hydration. Not to do so could be dehumanizing.

Yet some believe that withholding or withdrawing artificial nutrition
and hydration from those near death carries a distinctively weighty burden: it causes their death. We believe this position is misguided.[5] Rather
than causing death, withholding or withdrawing artificial nutrition and
hydration can be a way of accepting death. Those who are already
approaching death often stop eating and drinking. Not providing them
with artificial nutrition and hydration at this time, or withdrawing it, is
therefore consistent with the usual course of dying. It allows death to take
its ordinary course.

When artificial feeding is removed from those who are in the midst of
dying because it is useless or burdensome, a temporary barrier against
death is being ended and a person is being allowed—not caused—to die.
The underlying disease is finally being allowed to take its course toward
death. It is important to recognize that the cause of death is not necessarily the last thing that occurs immediately before it. Thus, when a man with
coronary artery disease who is progressively dying has a cardiac arrest and
the attempts of medical personnel to resuscitate him are to no avail or disproportionately burdensome, the cause of his death is not their cessation
of cardiopulmonary resuscitation, but the underlying heart disease. Similarly,
when artificial feeding is ended because its use would be to no avail or disproportionately burdensome, the cause of death should not be construed
as the removal of treatment, but the underlying condition of the patient.

*Discerning when artificial nutrition and hydration can be withheld or
withdrawn.* Resolving these issues with a specific person will call for a

process of moral discernment in which that person's good, the human ends and purposes of his or her life, are the primary considerations. Is continued medical intervention the most responsible use of power in this instance? Which course of treatment or nontreatment is most faithful to the call to continue right relationships between the dying person and his or her loved ones and with God? The patient, or those acting on behalf of the patient, will need to respond to these questions in a way that takes account of the unique purposes of that person, with all the complexities of thoughts, emotions, issues, and circumstances that characterize him or her.

By no means do we suggest that this will involve a utilitarian calculus in which benefits and burdens for all are totaled up with each person's interests counted as much as those of the patient. Rather, it will involve a weighing of benefits and burdens in a broad sense focused on the good of the patient as a member of the Christian community. It will also take into account the purposes of the patient, including the need to preserve those relationships that have been part of the warp and woof of his or her life. It will honor the form of life that he or she has treasured and wants to sustain, even as death approaches. Thus, the decision about the morally appropriate use of artificial nutrition and hydration will call for discernment of what ends and purposes should be honored in a person's dying. It will require asking whether we can further this person's unique journey toward God. These are weighty matters that we have a responsibility to address prayerfully, mindful of the love, concern, and grace of God.

HOSPICE, PALLIATIVE CARE, AND QUERIES ABOUT MORAL USES OF PAIN-RELIEVING DRUGS

It is perhaps no accident that the great renewal of care for the dying in the English-speaking world, the hospice movement, originated with the work of Dame Cicely Saunders, a physician and nurse whose sensibility has been deeply formed by Anglican practical piety. During the Middle Ages the term *hospice* was originated and referred to a way station for travelers; it was a place to stop for solace and refreshment before they continued their journey. Today, hospice refers to a way of assisting patients and families who are faced with the challenge of faithful dying. It is a way of caring for those near death primarily in their homes, and, to a lesser extent, in freestanding or institutionally affiliated hospice locations.

The hospice movement is dedicated to ensuring that people die in comfort, surrounded by the human family. Its basic goal is to provide comprehensive care that will achieve a good quality of life for each person by meeting his or her physical, emotional, social, and spiritual needs. Thus, the spiritual imperative to provide comfort care for the whole person near the end of life is at the very foundation of hospice. The principles that govern hospice care are to provide pain control at the end of life, to allow dying at home, and to avoid excessive use of medical technology that unnecessarily prolongs dying. Hospice also has a commitment to consider the families of patients as part of the unit of care.

Dr. Cicely Saunders, in discussing the impact of hospice on patients and caregivers, observes that:

> There are important ways in which we heal our patients, and in which they heal us. Healing a person does not always mean curing a disease. Sometimes healing means learning to care for others, finding new wholeness as a family—being reconciled. Or it can mean easing the pain of dying or allowing someone to die when the time comes. There is a difference between prolonging life and prolonging the act of dying until the patient lives a travesty of life.[6]

Hospice care can be tremendously helpful to patients who fear dying in pain and suffering and to families frightened and overwhelmed by the thought of taking care of someone they love who is dying on his or her own. Often, however, patients, families, and caregivers wait too long to contact hospice services because of a reluctance to acknowledge that death is on the horizon. Consequently, those who are offered this form of care are usually in the last phases of dying and have missed receiving this form of care earlier when it could have been of assistance to them and their families. We therefore urge patients, families, and professional caregivers to acknowledge the reality of the situation of those who are approaching death so that they can receive the kind of comfort and support that hospice can provide.

The time of faithful dying, for Christians, is a time in which to gather together the human family, not a time of isolation and abandonment. Thus, the hospice ideal fits well with the Anglican vision of the corporate nature of Christian faith and human life in which each person is an essential part of the community, a neighbor to be loved as ourselves. The hospice movement has contributed immeasurably to a worldwide effort to make death a gentle and accepted event, rather than a technical medical problem. Its efforts ought to be applauded and supported.

Need for hospice-like care for those in advanced stages of chronic illness. A problem arises for some who are in the advanced stages of chronic illness because they have a life expectancy greater than six months and are therefore not eligible for federally funded hospice care. Those who suffer from such conditions as dementia, stroke, heart disease, and chronic obstructive lung disease are on a course toward death whose end-point is difficult to predict. They will not necessarily die within six months. These patients could benefit from coordinated hospice-like care that is modified to meet their current and long-term needs. Such care would include not only the sort of physical, social, and spiritual support offered by hospice, but also some forms of acute care that are appropriate to their individual circumstances. Yet no such hospice-like care is available for them. Thus, these persons who are in the advanced stages of a chronic illness can face substantial pain and isolation as they die. Trial efforts are currently underway to develop and provide a program of hospice-like care to such patients.[7] The task force believes that our healthcare system needs to expand its notion of dying persons to include such chronically ill persons. We support these trial programs of mixed hospice and acute care for these persons and call on federal and state policy makers to support this form of care.

Need for greater efforts at pain relief. As this description of hospice care reveals, the relief of pain and suffering is a foremost consideration for those who are approaching the end of life. Pain attacks the body and the spirit. It can cripple the body so that seemingly ordinary tasks become a major ordeal or cannot be pursued at all. A patient's attention may focus so narrowly on the pain itself that other cares and spiritual purposes may be abandoned. Thus, as a physical and spiritual matter, the relief of pain is a primary purpose of medicine.

Professional and lay caregivers are called to offer a compassionate response to those who face such pain and suffering. Medicine has made major advances in the treatment of pain. It has learned much about appropriate use of narcotics to relieve pain in the dying, developed local anesthetic blocks to alleviate certain kinds of pain, and created multidisciplinary pain clinics to treat pain in the whole person. And yet, ironically, these advances have not been reaching a significant proportion of patients who are dying. In recent studies, a sizeable percentage of families surveyed reported that a dying member had spent the last two or three days of life in considerable pain.[8] As a consequence of such reports, medicine is now devoting greater attention to palliative care and pain relief as a way of averting this pain and suffering and providing support and comfort to those whose lives are near their end.

The importance of pain management, both physically and spiritually, cannot be overstated. When medicine and nursing can no longer hope to resolve an illness by means of aggressive treatment, professionals in these disciplines still have a role to play in attending to the needs and good of the whole person. They, along with several other disciplines, can offer palliative care. This is a significant component of a Christian response to those near the end of life. It is the sort of care that is provided by hospice.

In brief, *palliative care* refers generically to medical, surgical, and other procedures that are used to alleviate suffering, pain, discomfort, and dysfunction. It differs from typical medical interventions in that its goal is to provide comfort and relief from pain and suffering, rather than to cure an underlying disease. It includes pain control, as well as nurturing care settings, family support, care for "minor" symptoms such as nausea and dry lips, pastoral care, and many other practices that focus on the physical, emotional, and spiritual needs of the whole person. The management of pain in this context becomes a central expression of care for the person who is dying. To hear the call for relief from pain and to respond is to let another know that he or she matters and need not fear being isolated and abandoned in the face of pain.

Appropriate use of pain-relieving drugs near the end of life. There is some concern, however, about how aggressively physicians should seek pain relief when the drugs they provide for this purpose might also hasten death. Some conscientious health professionals resist raising narcotic dosages to the point where they are adequate to suppress pain, thinking that because these medications will suppress respiration, along with pain, they are the actual cause of death. Others fear that their patients will become addicted to the drugs they give to relieve pain. Still others hesitate to provide adequate pain relief out of fear of losing their licenses or of criminal charges. We believe that such stances are mistaken; their perspective is based on a misunderstanding of the facts of palliative care, the morality of the acts involved, and the legal regulation of the use of pain-relieving drugs.

In the vast majority of cases, appropriate pain relief can be given by healthcare professionals in ways that do not place patients at risk of a hastened death. Indeed, it often happens that increased doses of pain-relieving drugs have the effect of extending, rather than shortening, patients' lives. This is because people who are comfortable are more apt to accept greater nourishment and less likely to lose energy to the stress of pain. Thus they tend to live longer in relative comfort.

When this is not the case and the use of a gradually increased dose of narcotic leads to an earlier death, it is misleading to say that the administration of these pain-relieving drugs is the cause of death. The cause of death, as we observed above in the discussion of artificial nutrition and hydration, is not necessarily the last thing that happens to a person before death. When a person dies a few hours or days earlier as a result of the administration of pain-relieving drugs, the cause of that person's death is not the administration of these drugs, but the underlying lethal condition. This is the accepted moral and legal view.

To explain the morality of this and other situations in which an act will have at least two outcomes, one good and the other bad, moral theologians over the centuries have developed the *principle of double effect.* When the proper conditions are met, the principle of double effect says that it is morally acceptable to act in order to bring about the good effect, even though this will allow the foreseen bad outcome to occur. The person acting in the case covered by the principle does not aim at the bad outcome, but acquiesces in allowing it to occur. The agent, however, must be sure that the good outcome morally outweighs the bad one, that there is no other way to bring about the good outcome, and that the bad outcome does not cause the good one.

For example, the surgeon who operates on a patient with the aim of removing a cancerous growth foresees that this will create postoperative pain but does not act in order to bring that pain about; therefore, the principle of double effect indicates, this surgery is morally acceptable. In the same way, when narcotics are provided to alleviate pain and suffering in a dying person and this may decrease the rate of respiration and allow death to arrive sooner, the principle of double effect indicates that the use of these narcotics is morally acceptable. The hospice caregiver foresees that the patient may have an earlier death but does not intend this. The alleviation of pain and suffering in the dying is a morally good outcome that outweighs the unintended side effect of an earlier death.[9]

To be sure, there is such a thing as an excessively high dosage that necessarily leads to death. This is a dosage that physicians have been called by their profession and the law not to provide. Deliberately giving an excessive dose of a drug, however, is very different from responsibly increasing dosages of medication to a point needed in order to keep persons free from pain. Hospice physicians have learned that they can give gradually increased doses of narcotics to dying patients until these reach a very high level, and yet not decrease respiration and hasten their patients' death. This suggests that the distinction between a high dose that is within the realm of appropriate pain relief and a high dose that is excessive must be drawn carefully so as not to discourage physicians from appropriately prescribing gradually larger doses of pain-relieving medication. Professional caregivers who titrate the use of narcotics to alleviate pain in the dying according to the accepted standards of medical and hospice care should not fear loss of their license or criminal charges.[10] Indeed, the Supreme Court of the United States in 1997, according to a respected legal commentator, "effectively required all states to ensure that their laws do not obstruct the provision of adequate palliative care, especially for the alleviation of pain and other physical symptoms of people facing death."[11] Thus, there is strong legal support for the professional provision of adequate pain-relieving drugs near the end of life.

Moreover, professional caregivers and families need not fear causing patients to become addicted to narcotics. The Hastings Center, a respected medical ethics educational and research organization, has indicated that:

> Health care professionals and families are also sometimes concerned that dying patients may become addicted to narcotics; professionals consequently tend to provide insufficient doses. This concern arises from a confusion between physical and psychological dependence and from a

misunderstanding of the dangers each poses for dying patients. People who are physically dependent experience distressing symptoms if narcotics are suddenly withdrawn. Those who are psychologically dependent desire drugs and become driven to obtain them. Physical dependence regularly occurs in dying patients, but psychological dependence is rare. Physical dependence does not trouble those who are dying, for the administration of narcotics need never end abruptly and cause them distress . . . Since psychological dependence is rare, health care professionals should address the problem on those few occasions when it occurs rather than allow the majority of dying patients to suffer out of a misplaced fear of psychological dependence.[12]

Appropriate use of total sedation. Modern pain control does not, in most cases, require rendering people unconscious but allows them to remain aware, even as their pain is diminished. Sometimes, however, the only way to suppress pain or to relieve other forms of suffering, such as shortness of breath, agitation, or severe anxiety, is to use analgesia to the point of unconsciousness. The purpose of this *total sedation,* as it should be called, is to make the patient unaware of symptoms that cannot be eliminated or satisfactorily controlled by other forms of clinical intervention.[13] Such sedation is sought only rarely, but when it is needed, it presents a difficult issue for Anglican ethics with its focus on the social character of human life. Patients who receive total sedation suffer the loss of consciousness and with that the ability to know, to act, and to relate to others. Their pain may be relieved, but they may not then be able to listen to the surrounding world, to say what they want to say to those they love, to make final decisions about their own life, or to pray and commend themselves to God. Conscious relationship is extremely important in the Christian life. Total sedation has the effect of leaving the patient present and yet not present—or perhaps present in a very different way from before. So the choice for the patient seems to be between discomfort, distraction, and pain on the one hand, and absence and limbo on the other. Yet total sedation need not be permanent. It can be lightened to allow a patient to return to a state of consciousness. In most instances, it is medically and morally appropriate continually to reassess the patient's status and to lessen sedation when this is appropriate. Arrangements for a period of lucidity need to be made with the patient beforehand in such cases.

We see no reason that total sedation may not be chosen by patients who are able to decide for themselves or by family or other designated decision makers when patients are unable to decide for themselves. Rest and peace are cherished states in Christian tradition, and they are certainly permissible at the end of life. When we must choose for another who is decisionally incapacitated and find that total sedation is the only way that we can relieve that person's pain, much better that than nothing. Family, friends, and professional caregivers who are keeping company with a person who can no longer respond due to total sedation may find it difficult to keep their watch. These concerned persons who must stand by as the unconscious person moves toward death also need special support at this time.

Perhaps the most problematical instance of total sedation occurs when the question arises of whether to withhold or withdraw artificial nutrition and hydration at the same time. These two questions are distinct. The issue of whether to provide total sedation is medically and morally different from that of whether to provide artificial feeding; therefore, the two practices should be considered separately.

Finally, we recognize that the desire of a person near death who wishes to seek reconciliation with God and others can have certain implications for the timing of the use of pain-relieving drugs. Some of those approaching death may want to be able to speak with others, to pray, to take Communion, and to witness to their faith. Yet they may be experiencing tremendous pain and suffering that leaves them unable to focus sufficiently to carry out these significant plans. These patients, therefore, may want the option of retaining a certain level of consciousness, knowing that this means they will endure some pain.[14] When this is the case, medical caregivers can usually titrate the medication to avoid sedating the patient to the point of unconsciousness. Although the Anglican tradition does not require anyone to die in relievable pain, neither does it deny to those near death, who so choose, the spiritual opportunity for reconciliation and for the expression of faith, even if this entails that they will experience some pain.

WHETHER PHYSICIAN-ASSISTED SUICIDE IS A PRACTICE WE SHOULD EMBRACE

Before we consider the poignant and divisive question of physician-assisted suicide, it is important to make clear what we mean by it so that we do not misunderstand what is at issue.

Suicide is an act in which a person intentionally takes his or her own life. The person who commits suicide (1) acts by his or her own hand in order to bring about death and (2) intends to cause death. Death is this person's objective, the end that he or she intends to reach. In contrast, when Christian martyrs die because they refuse to renounce their faith, they do not commit suicide, for no act of theirs brings about their death and they do not refuse intending to be killed. Their convictions force them to face and accept death, but this is a consequence they would avoid if they could do so without violating their conscience.

It is important to point out that *there is a moral difference between committing suicide and stopping treatment near the end of life.* When a patient decides that treatment, such as resuscitation in the event of a cardiac arrest, would be futile and overly burdensome and subsequently dies when a cardiac arrest occurs, that patient has not committed suicide. He or she has not brought about death by his or her own hand and has not acted with the intention of causing death.

In *assisted suicide,* one person intentionally gives another the means to take his or her own life at the latter's request. In *physician-assisted suicide,* a physician gives a patient a drug or other medical means of ending his or her life in order that the patient may bring about his or her own death.

Euthanasia is distinct from assisted suicide. It has come to mean that one person causes the death of another who is terminally or seriously ill, often in order to end the latter's pain and suffering. Euthanasia requires the explicit intent to end another's life.

Some see physician-assisted suicide as a compassionate response to those approaching death who are in pain and suffering.[15] They believe that it is better to assist patients to end their lives than have them go through a miserable period of dying. Physicians, they hold, have a special responsibility to provide this form of assistance because they have pledged to care for their patients and have the specialized knowledge to give them doses of drugs that will bring about their death with certainty and with little or no attendant suffering. Others, however, see physician-assisted suicide as a way of isolating and abandoning those who are near death, a way of fleeing from compassion for them rather than expressing it.

The Christian tradition has consistently opposed taking one's own life. However, it has also acknowledged that for each of us a point may well come when we have reached the "time to die" spoken of in Ecclesiastes. At that time, we should accept that we need not receive life-sustaining treatment. The Christian tradition stresses the differences in both actions and intentions between directly ending our lives and refraining from having further futile or burdensome treatment. The task force believes the tradition is correct in affirming this distinction.

Arguments for physician-assisted suicide. Two arguments have given particular strength to the contemporary case for physician-assisted suicide. The first recognizes that our society has a healthy respect for human autonomy and privacy, especially where intimate and deeply personal matters are at issue. We believe that individuals have a right to control the shape of their lives and to resist intrusions into the decisions they make about choice of career, spouse, or reproduction. Similarly, those presenting this argument believe, a person's death is his or her business. People should be free to die as they want, and if they elect to die with the assistance of physicians, that choice should be honored.

Moreover, they maintain that as Christians we have reason to take the claims of autonomy and privacy seriously. An essential element of the image of God that we bear is our ability to choose freely, to initiate voluntary and intentional acts. Thus, a central aspect of human dignity lies in our capacity to direct our lives. Advocates of physician-assisted suicide argue that this God-given capacity means that we can choose to end our lives when we are in great pain and suffering and can no longer serve God or others. Physician-assisted suicide, on this approach, expresses respect for the choice of an individual to end his or her life when it is no longer possible to achieve those purposes for which that individual was brought into the world.

A second distinct argument for assisted suicide is based on the common perception that dying in the modern world can be protracted, painful, and uncomfortable. This perception is not a total delusion. As we noted above in the discussion of palliative care and pain relief, it is based on people's observations of the occasionally miserable deaths of some of their family and friends. Those considering suicide may be concerned not only about dying in pain but may feel abandoned and overwhelmed by affliction because their needs and human purposes have not been met. Against this dehumanization at the end of life, physician-assisted suicide seems to offer the hope of averting suffering of a kind that can utterly destroy the person.

This concern is at the foundation of the rationale for suicide offered by certain authors.[16] In some unusual instances, they believe, the continuing burden of suffering experienced by a person near the end of life can be so great that the integrity and identity of the self is threatened or lost. When this occurs, affliction turns to resentment, anger, and, finally, bitterness. Relationships with God and neighbor are destroyed. The situations these authors have in mind are rare but are such that a decision to take one's own life may be morally justifiable, they believe.

This is not to make suicide a norm, that is, not a moral decision that a person should make in the normal course of dying. Rather, suicide may be morally justified, on this view, only in exceptional and extreme situations where pain management is difficult or impossible or where the course of the disease is so debilitating that it threatens bodily integrity and the ends and values of life itself. Such a view is not contrary to Christian faith, these authors hold, for Christian faith does not resolve these difficult and exceptional circumstances and questions. It calls us into life to give reverence to it by honoring and caring for it as given in relationship to God. Life is a gift. We are called into life that we may live. Yet life is not another god to be maintained in the face of extreme suffering. In those rare circumstances in which such suffering would destroy the integrity of the person to whom God has given life, these authors find that suicide can be a morally appropriate act.

Those who favor suicide in such instances are quick to point out that this does not imply approval of socially sanctioned assisted suicide. The question of suicide by an individual in exceptional instances is distinct from that of legally approved assisted suicide, they hold. To make assisted suicide a normal and accepted decision within society would be to sanction the taking of human life as a matter of social policy. This would undercut the sense of the primary importance of human life that is essential to the continued survival and flourishing of society. While individuals in the extreme circumstances described above may choose to take their own lives without moral condemnation, according to those taking this approach, socially approved assisted suicide is another matter.

Arguments against physician-assisted suicide. Despite these powerful arguments for assisted suicide, others within the Christian tradition have continued to oppose this act both in individual cases and as a socially accepted practice. They have offered several significant arguments for their opposition based on our relations with one another and with God.

The first of these arguments against assisted suicide relates to the social character of the human self. The self, as we know it, is a creature of society. The development of our self begins as we articulate the voices of those around us. We are a child, sister, friend, lover, or parent of particular individuals. These relations are not accidental characteristics of our lives but are of our essence, as F. D. Maurice argued in the nineteenth century.[17] We are more than the sum of these human relations; we are never isolated creatures for whom being related to others is simply a matter of choice. We are essentially social creatures. God created nothing simply for itself. As we have described Anglican understandings of Christian faith, life is given corporately as we share in one body. A view of the self that sees all engagements with others as negotiable, contingent matters of choice is mistaken. On this approach, suicide is seldom, if ever, strictly a "self-regarding" or private act with no implications for others but is, to the contrary, an extraordinarily powerful, indeed an unanswerable, social act. Its social repercussions can be enormous. Families and friends of those who commit suicide must live with the emotional consequences for the rest of their lives.

This said, at times, some persons have thought of ending their own lives for the sake of others, or in a context of deep and protracted despair. The immediate causes are varied: the fear of being a burden to one's family or of expending resources carefully saved for others; the hopelessness of a diagnosis or the fear of becoming demented or further incapacitated. Love, despair, and fear of weakness are powerful motivations, and they can point to suicide as the most efficient way out.

Whatever immediate reasons may be given, there is a significant association between depression and a desire for assisted suicide; this suggests that it is not necessarily a carefully reasoned choice.[18] Even when reasons for suicide appear persuasive, they are often inadequately informed. Due to depression, they may fail to take into consideration the complexity of

our relations with others and our responsibilities to those we believe we
would burden by our presence. A fear of being dependent on others, even
those who are loved and who return that love, pushes some to consider
suicide. Yet those they want to spare the labor and tedium of care for them
overlook that these relatives and friends can gain a heightened sense of
meaning and purpose in tending to them. Indeed, as Dr. Cicely Saunders
has said: "The often surprising potential for personal and family growth at
this stage is one of the strongest objections most hospice workers feel for
the legalization of a deliberately hastened death . . ."[19]

A second reason to reject suicide near the end of life is that the social
impact of allowing physician-assisted suicide is immense. The bishops at
Lambeth in 1998 perceived that allowing assisted suicide and euthanasia
would create "[a] diminution of respect for all human life, especially of the
marginalised and those who may be regarded as 'unproductive' members
of society." They expressed concern about "the potential devaluing of
worth, in their own eyes, of the elderly, the sick and of those who are
dependent on others for their well being."[20] This was also a concern of the
United States Supreme Court when it rejected a constitutional right to
assisted suicide in 1997.[21] Were assisted suicide to be legalized and become
an accepted practice, the assumption would become that those who are
old, sick, and disabled should take the opportunity, offered to them by
society, to end it all. The question, "Why aren't you dead yet?" would
become an accepted query to the weakest and most vulnerable among us.[22]
Thus, the validation of assisted suicide by law could create a social ethos in
which the sick, disabled, and dying would be expected either to justify their
existence or to kill themselves.

A third serious concern has been raised about physician-assisted suicide: to make doctors accomplices in the suicide of patients would erode
trust in these healthcare professionals. The Committee on Medical Ethics
of the Diocese of Washington points out that opponents of physician-
assisted suicide maintain that "[t]aking human life is antithetical to the
work of healing and relieving suffering that is essential to the role of the
physician."[23] For doctors to assist patients to take their lives is contrary to
the long-standing physician ethic of healing. Patients might have reason to
fear that physicians who consider it licit to provide them with lethal doses
of drugs might take it upon themselves to administer such doses without
patient consultation at times that they deem this appropriate.

Assisted suicide is opposed within the Anglican tradition not only
because it fails to honor the social, corporate character of our lives but for
more pointedly theological reasons as well. It puts into question our relationship with one another and also challenges our relationship with God.
The English lawyer Blackstone called suicide "hurrying into the presence
of the Almighty uncalled for."[24] The idea that taking life represents a

usurpation of God's sovereignty has been a central argument against suicide in theological ethics. A 1975 Anglican Working Group stated about the Christian that "he can claim no inalienable right to death on the grounds that his life is his own and that after due consideration has been given to the interests of other men and women, he may do with it exactly as he pleases."[25] Some who present this view see God as sovereign; others see God as loving parent. The former portray suicide as disobeying One who is our owner, whereas the latter see it as offending and hurting God. Both view a life of response to God and others as one that is not completely under the control of oneself, but rather is lived in relationship with God and others. Acceptance, patience, and endurance are at the heart of such a life.

Our relationship with God qualifies and informs our relationships with one another. Yet we are never simply products of those relationships. The different and individualizing factor comes with our relationship with God. At times, God may seem absent or hostile. Such estrangement from God is a component of every human life, and we sometimes find we approach this absent Other with distrust or dread. But Christians are bold to say that this is not the norm, that God is present and to be trusted—indeed, to be loved. When we affirm the trustworthiness and love of God we implicitly affirm the goodness of our lives—as God's gift and as God's children. This conviction of God's care for us is central to our tradition and worship, nowhere more clearly than in our conviction of God's identification with us in Christ.

Suicide has been seen as a breach in our relationship with God because it seeks to substitute control by the self for the initiative of God and to treat the gift of life as something other than a gift. The illusion of control keeps the threat of dependence at bay, but it is only that—an illusion. Honest appraisal of our situation reveals the limits of our power. It also reveals the greatness of God's love. Responding to that love and feeling gratitude for the gift of life need not mean living as long as possible. At the end of life, the love and generosity of God constrain the way in which we choose to see our lives close. There comes a time when each of us should be willing to surrender our lives to God. We may do so by rightly choosing to refuse treatment. But discernment that medical treatment may only be prolonging the process of dying should be distinguished from insisting that each of us must be in charge of our dying. That insistence shows a misunderstanding of reality: that the self is loved by and is a child of God.

Final task force reflections on physician-assisted suicide. We join in the concern, expressed with compassion by those who favor physician-assisted suicide, for those near death who are in extreme pain and suffering. The Church has never valorized the suffering of the sick and dying as a good to be embraced for its own sake. Although it recognizes that some suffering is part of the human condition, it has attempted to overcome the suffering of those approaching death by actively caring for them and offering prayers for their healing. In this, it has followed the lead of Jesus, who healed the sick and wept for the dead.

There are those who die today in extreme pain and suffering. The End of Life Task Force does not support the cruel extension of such suffering but instead calls out for its alleviation. Where there are drugs available to hand to a despairing person near death so that he or she can commit suicide, there are also drugs available to provide to that person that will afford relief from pain and allow a peaceful death. And such drugs, along with other palliative measures, are available for the relief from pain today.[26] Hence, there should be no need for anyone to undergo radical suffering near the end of life. The way in which to address such terrible suffering is to eliminate it, rather than eliminate the persons who undergo it.

Members of the task force therefore believe that the Episcopal Church should continue to oppose suicide near the end of life.[27] We have no desire to go back to a time in which suicide was thought of as an unforgivable sin, nor do we wish to attempt to pass judgment on those who make this choice as a matter of faithfulness to God, given their particular situation.[28] However, for the reasons given above, we think that suicide should be rejected as a norm for the Christian life. In addition, members of the task force oppose physician-assisted suicide. Such a practice risks making suicide a norm rather than an exceptional act. Support for physician-assisted suicide not only departs from the teaching of the Christian tradition but is in our view unnecessary, given our ability to provide palliative care even to the point of total sedation. Moreover, physician-assisted suicide may lead to public policy that is highly problematical and risky.

To summarize our reflections in this chapter, we draw together the following observations and conclusions. The agonizing choices made at the end of life should always occur in a spirit of fear and trembling. No one should claim confidently to know the state of someone else's mind or another person's intentions. Although artificial nutrition and hydration are significant forms of treatment because of their close association with caring and feeding, the End of Life Task Force believes that they can be withheld or withdrawn when individuals are approaching death and their use would be burdensome and contrary to human purposes. Further, the task force stresses the importance of effective palliative care and spiritual and social support near the end of life. We maintain that doses of pain-relieving medicine should be raised to the point of efficacy when that is what patients or families request. Dying need not and should not be a time of such pain and despair that patients are led to kill themselves. We oppose socially sanctioned physician-assisted suicide and urgently call for the provision of adequate and appropriate palliative care for those who are approaching death.

Indeed, it is a judgment against the community and its failure to address and support dying persons that some die today with inadequate palliation, human and spiritual support, and comfort. The End of Life Task Force unequivocally and militantly insists that the practices, financing patterns, and habits that allow miserable dying to continue to be a reality in the United States and around the world must be changed. This is particularly important at a time when forms of financing and the provision of medical care are in flux and there is enormous social pressure to limit costs. Physician-assisted suicide, proposed as a strategy for empowering individuals, can easily evolve into a practice that efficiently simplifies and rationalizes care at the end of life in a cost-effective way. We do not want to create a world in which people have the options of either a terrible and expensive death or a thrifty physician-assisted suicide. We can offer them something better—care and support to ease their way at the end of life.

Many aspects of being critically ill and dying are beyond human control. Dying involves an inevitable loss of control over our bodies, much of the world that surrounds us, and many of our social relations. Yet we can affect many other aspects of our own dying. Participating in our care can offer us an opportunity to have an impact on our bodies, our world, and our personal relations. The Anglican tradition has affirmed the importance of the responsible use of our freedom to choose. Nowhere does this freedom become more important than in the setting where we make decisions about the form that our treatment will—or will not—take. In the next chapter, we acknowledge the importance of human freedom of choice within the healthcare setting as a sign of the great value and responsibility that God has bestowed on us and offer ways to exercise it responsibly near the end of life.

---

1. Karl Barth, *Church Dogmatics,* vol. III, section 4, 357–363, reprinted in *On Moral Medicine: Theological Perspectives in Medical Ethics,* 2nd ed., ed. Stephen E. Lammers and Allen Verhey (Grand Rapids, Mich.: Eerdmans, 1998), 7–12.

2. The bishops at the Lambeth Conference of 1998 took a similar position with regard to the use of artificial feeding in those who are in a persistent vegetative state, declaring, "When a person is in a permanent vegetative state, to sustain him or her with artificial nutrition and hydration may be seen as constituting medical intervention." *The Official Report of the Lambeth Conference, 1998,* "Called to Full Humanity. Section 1 Report. Theme 5: Euthanasia," (Harrisburg, Pa.: Morehouse, 1999), 101–106, 104. For further discussion of permanent or persistent vegetative state, see Committee on Medical Ethics, Episcopal Diocese of Washington, *Toward a Good Christian Death: Crucial Treatment Choices* (Harrisburg, Pa.: Morehouse, 1999), 49–50 and "Appendix A. Distinguishing Several Sorts of Prolonged Unconsciousness from Brain Death," 115–118.

3. Joyce V. Zerwekh, "Do Dying Patients Really Need IV Fluids?" *American Journal of Nursing,* 1997, vol. 97, No. 3, 26–30; R. N. McCann, et al., "Comfort Care for Terminally Ill Patients: The Appropriate Use of Nutrition and Hydration," *Journal of the American Medical Association,* 1994, vol. 272, 1263–1266.

4. J. E. Ellershaw, et al., "Dehydration and the Dying Patient," *Journal of Pain and Symptom Management*, 1995, vol. 10, 192–197; L. A. Printz, "Terminal Dehydration, A Compassionate Treatment," *Archives of Internal Medicine*, 1992, vol. 152, 697–700; R. J. Sullivan, "Accepting Death without Artificial Nutrition or Hydration," *Journal of General Internal Medicine*, 1993, vol. 8, 220–224.

5. Daniel Callahan, "Commentary: Too Sick to Eat: The Case of Joseph," *Casebook on the Termination of Life-Sustaining Treatment and Care of the Dying*, ed. Cynthia B. Cohen (Bloomington, Ind.: Indiana University Press, 1988), 55–58.

6. Sandol Stoddard, *The Hospice Movement: A Better Way of Caring for the Dying* (New York: Vintage, 1992), 91.

7. Joanne Lynn, "Caring at the End of Our Lives," *New England Journal of Medicine*, vol. 335, No. 3, 1996, 201–202.

8. The SUPPORT Principal Investigators, "A Controlled Trial to Improve Care for Seriously Ill Hospitalized Patients: The Study to Understand Prognoses and Preferences for Outcomes and Risks of Treatment (SUPPORT)," *Journal of the American Medical Association*, 1995, vol. 274, 1591–1598; Joanne Lynn, Joan Teno, R. S. Phillips, et al., "Perceptions by Family Members of the Dying Experience of Older and Seriously Ill Patients," *Annals of Internal Medicine*, 1997, vol. 126, No. 2, 97–106.

9. Some maintain that there is no moral difference between intending to bring about an outcome and foreseeing that that outcome will occur and therefore hold that the principle of double effect is invalid for this and other reasons. For further discussion, see Committee on Medical Ethics, Episcopal Diocese of Washington, *Assisted Suicide and Euthanasia: Christian Moral Perspectives, "The Washington Report"* (Harrisburg, Pa.: Morehouse, 1997), 16–18.

10. Sandra H. Johnson, "Disciplinary Actions and Pain Relief: Analysis of the Pain Relief Act," *Journal of Law, Medicine & Ethics*, 1996, vol. 24, No. 4, 319–327; Chris Stern Hyman, "Pain Management and Disciplinary Action: How State Medical Boards Can Remove Barriers to Effective Treatment," *Journal of Law, Medicine & Ethics*, 1996, vol. 24, No. 4, 328–337; David E. Joranson and Aaron M. Gilson, "Improving Pain Management through Policy Making and Education for Medical Regulators," *Journal of Law, Medicine & Ethics*, 1996, vol. 24, No. 4, 338–343. Robyn S. Shapiro, "Health Care Providers' Liability Exposure for Inappropriate Pain Management," *Journal of Law, Medicine & Ethics*, 1996, vol. 24, No. 4, 348–359.

11. Robert A. Burt, "The Supreme Court Speaks: Not Assisted Suicide but a Constitutional Right to Palliative Care," *New England Journal of Medicine*, 1997, vol. 337, No. 17, 1234–1236.

12. Susan M. Wolf, Cynthia B. Cohen, Bruce Jennings, Paul Homer, Daniel Callahan, and The Hastings Center Study Group, *Guidelines on the Termination of Life-Sustaining Treatment and the Care of the Dying* (Bloomington, Ind.: Indiana University, 1987), 72.

13. N. I. Cherny and R. K. Portenoy, "Sedation in the Management of Refractory Symptoms: Guidelines for Evaluation and Treatment," *Journal of Palliative Care*, 1994, vol. 10, 31–38.

14. We are indebted to Rev. Dr. Charles Price, professor emeritus at Virginia Theological Seminary, for pointing this out to us.

15. For this position, see "Report of the Task Force on Assisted Suicide to the 122nd Convention of the Episcopal Diocese of Newark," January, 1996; for a discussion of the pros and cons of the question, see Committee on Medical Ethics, Diocese of Washington, *Assisted Suicide and Euthanasia*.

16. James F. Gustafson, *Ethics from a Theocentric Perspective*, vol. 2 (Chicago: University of Chicago Press, 1984), 187–216; Lisa Sowle Cahill, "A 'Natural Law' Reconsideration of Euthanasia," in *On Moral Medicine: Theological Perspectives in Medical Ethics*, 1st ed., ed. Stephen E. Lammers and Allen Verhey (Grand Rapids, Mich.: Eerdmans, 1987), 445–453.

17. F. D. Maurice, *The Kingdom of Christ*, vol. 1, 228.

18. E. J. Emanuel, D. L. Fairclough, E. R. Daniels, and B. R. Clarridge, "Euthanasia and Physician-Assisted Suicide: Attitudes and Experiences of Oncology Patients, Oncologists, and

the Public," *Lancet,* 1996, vol. 347, 1805–1810; W. Breibart, B. D. Rosenfeld, and S. D. Passik, "Interest in Physician-Assisted Suicide among Ambulatory HIV-Infected Patients, *American Journal of Psychiatry,* 1996, vol. 153, 238–242; H.M. Chochinov, K. G. Wilson, M. Enns, N. Mowchun, S. Lander, M. Levitt, and J. J. Clinch, "Desire for Death in the Terminally Ill," *American Journal of Psychiatry,* 1995, vol. 152, 1185–1191.

19. Cicely Saunders, "On Dying Well," *The Cambridge Review,* February, 1984, 27.

20. *The Official Report of the Lambeth Conference,* 1998, 104.

21. *Washington v. Glucksberg,* 117 S. Ct. 2258 (1997); *Vacco v. Quill,* 117 S. Ct. 2293 (1997).

22. See Committee on Medical Ethics, Episcopal Diocese of Washington, *Assisted Suicide and Euthanasia,* 52.

23. Ibid., 54.

24. William Blackstone, *Commentary on the Laws of England,* vol. 4 (Chicago: University of Chicago Press, 1979), 189.

25. General Synod Board for Social Responsibility, *On Dying Well: An Anglican Contribution to the Debate on Euthanasia* (Newport and London: Church Information Office, 1975), 16.

26. Ira R. Byock, "Consciously Walking the Fine Line: Thoughts on a Hospice Response to Assisted Suicide and Euthanasia," *Journal of Palliative Care,* 1993, vol. 9, No. 3, 25–28; R. D. Truog, C. B. Berde, C. Mitchell, and H. E. Grier, "Barbiturates in the Care of the Terminally Ill," *New England Journal of Medicine,* 1992, vol. 327, No. 23, 1678–1681; R. D. Truog, and C. B. Berde, "Pain, Euthanasia, and Anesthesiologists," *Anesthesiology,* 1993, vol. 78, No. 2, 353–360.

27. See point 2 of the resolution, "Establish Principles with Regard to the Prolongation of Life," of the Seventieth General Convention of 1991, reprinted in Committee on Medical Ethics, Episcopal Diocese of Washington, *Toward a Good Christian Death,* 127.

28. Karl Barth, *Church Dogmatics,* translated by A. T. Mackay, et al. (Edinburgh: T & T Clark, 1961), vol. III. section 4, 404–411.

CHAPTER 5

MAKING RESPONSIBLE TREATMENT CHOICES

Our call to use our medical powers in ways that express the Anglican moral vision provided the focus of the last chapter. There it became clear that we have the power today to exercise considerable control over the time and manner of our deaths through the use or the withdrawal of life-sustaining treatment. It also became clear that when we are terminally ill or in the advanced stages of a chronic illness, we cannot avoid having to make difficult decisions about our treatment. Often, to decide not to make such decisions when we are in such conditions and circumstances is, in effect, to make a decision—it is to decide to continue whatever treatment is under way or not to begin some other treatment.

Yet the Anglican conviction is that we are called to use our medical powers responsibly. This means that we have a responsibility to evaluate when it would be right to have treatment and when treatment would be too burdensome or contrary to human purposes and, therefore, not morally required for us to use. Such assessments of how to use medical powers for ourselves or for someone we love are among the most difficult that we have to make. Three issues that are especially relevant to making such responsible healthcare choices emerge for discussion in this chapter: respect for persons, truth telling within the doctor-patient relationship, and the use of advance directives to guide care near the end of life.

RESPECT FOR PERSONS AND THEIR DECISIONS

The Anglican tradition recognizes that adults with the capacity to make decisions have the right and responsibility to make healthcare choices for themselves and for their children. They not only have the right to choose among treatment options but also have the right to refuse available treatments. These rights and responsibilities are grounded in what the bishops of the 1998 Lambeth Conference referred to as one of the "bedrock principles" of the Anglican Communion: "Human beings, while flawed by sin, nevertheless have the capacity to make free and responsible moral choices."[1] As creatures of God, we are called to use responsibly the freedom bestowed on us. Morcover, others have an obligation to acknowledge our freedom. This means not only that others ought to respect our freely made choices but that they also should respect us as persons.

For this reason, the Seventieth General Convention of the Episcopal Church declared that "the decision to withhold or withdraw life-sustaining treatment should ultimately rest with the patient, or with the patient's surrogate decision makers in the case of a mentally incapacitated patient."[2] This principle, part of a set of principles concerning the prolongation of life by means of life-sustaining treatment, further states that "the responsibility of individuals to reach informed decisions in this matter is acknowledged and honored."

It is important to note that the Church bodies cited here chose to use the language of responsibility, as well as that of rights, in their statements. This is a significant expression of the fundamental orientation of Anglicanism toward individual persons as bound in community with others and responsible to them. The Anglican tradition does not view us as isolated entities who must protect ourselves from others by claiming rights against them. Instead, it is a corporate faith that sees us as intimately bound together in community, with responsibility not only for decisions about our own person but also for how these decisions will affect others.

In some secular ethics literature, the respect owed to individuals is justified in terms of autonomy, or the right to decide for oneself. That surely captures part of what the Church has meant to affirm—but only a part. The task force resists the possible implication that anything that individuals freely choose is as good as another, as if morality were grounded only in the will of the human person, rather than ultimately in the will of God. As children of God, our task is to use our freedom in a responsible way, in a way that promotes our good and the good of others and that is responsive to God's purpose for us. Each of us may walk freely on the journey that is the moral life, but we walk with a compass and a direction, not aimlessly or arbitrarily. Thus, the Anglican tradition sets autonomy within the context of our relationship with God and others, stressing not only the freedom to choose, but the freedom to choose in ways that are rooted in our lives in community and in God's purposes.[3]

SPEAKING THE TRUTH TO PATIENTS

Anglicans recognize the moral and medical need to speak responsibly to those whose life is drawing to a close. They begin with the conviction that health professionals should speak openly and forthrightly with patients about their condition and treatment options. Both honesty (accurately speaking what one thinks to be the truth) and candor (volunteering information of clear relevance even when not asked for) are important in medical care for many reasons.

A primary reason for honesty and candor is that we, as patients, cannot carry out our responsibility to make decisions about our treatment without accurate information. Such information, in most healthcare settings, and particularly for those who face life-limiting illnesses, comes from healthcare providers. These caregivers are obligated to tell patients the truth about their conditions, inform them of the risks and benefits of available procedures or treatment regimens, and give them the opportunity to give or to withhold their consent. This requires a commitment to full disclosure in a way that takes account of the individual patient's worldview, cultural background, and moral framework.

Patients also need to be told the truth because honest communication among persons is a fundamental component of the Christian life. The practical piety of an Anglican way of life is deeply relational and calls upon believers concerned about right relationships to make truth a hallmark of their lives. Unless we acknowledge the dignity, personhood, and status of others as neighbors to be dealt with openly and honestly, we fail in our duty to promote right relationships with others. This broader view of truth telling suggests that honesty is but one component of truthful relationships; personal commitment and dedication are also essential to them. Truthful relationships of necessity involve personal investment in others.

In the context of the provision of healthcare, this fuller meaning of truth should inform the patient-caregiver relationship. In order to speak truthfully to patients, caregivers must establish relationships marked by trust and care. Healthcare professionals have recognized this over the past quarter century, as their professed ideals have evolved from an ethic of compassionate concealment to one of disclosure. We celebrate this significant change. It is no longer acceptable to allow the sad and unsettling news of grave illness to justify withholding such information.

But there are important issues of timing and wording that revolve around how caregivers communicate troubling news. Caregivers intent on "speaking the truth in love" (Ephesians 4:15) will recall that one can utter words that are accurate in ways that can terrify or estrange a vulnerable person. To do so is to betray a commitment to truth telling and also to violate the obligations enunciated earlier to use power responsibly, nurture right relationships, and promote human well being at the end of life. For example, we regard it as scandalous for a health professional to say, "I can do nothing more for you," even if there is nothing more to be done in terms of surgical or other narrowly medicinal cure. At the level of factual accuracy, the statement is simply false, because there is always more that can be done in the way of palliative care and support. Moreover, this sort of statement is troubling not only because it is false, but also because it may be perceived by the patient as indicating the professional's desire to break off the relationship and, in effect, to abandon the patient rather than walk the last mile with him or her.

The distinction between honestly reporting what one knows when asked and candidly volunteering facts of clear relevance that may not be asked for is of great moral importance. Professionals and families should be prepared to offer full disclosure to patients, but they should also be alert to signals, sometimes explicit, sometimes implicit, that a specific patient would prefer not to know every detail. Not everyone wants to know everything, nor is choosing not to know a sign of intellectual or moral weakness. To be sure, the burden of proof is on a choice not to know, but that burden of proof can sometimes be met.

The need to be sensitive to our relational as well as our informational needs may be particularly important outside a generalized Anglo and middle-class culture. Health professionals and others should be conscious of differences among the cultures within which patients have been nurtured. Varying social experiences may lead some groups and individual patients to place a different emphasis on truth telling from those who are immersed in mainstream American culture. Although individuals who have been shaped by particular cultures should not be stereotyped and assumed to accept the mores of their culture, we should not underestimate how powerfully social or cultural factors may inform their decision-making process at the end of life.[4] A cultural practice that considers it wrong to tell persons near death about their condition, but believes that instead families should be told, ought to be respected if that practice is clearly honored by patients and families.[5] Patients from cultures that view it as harmful to disclose bad news because this diminishes hope and individual thriving and who indicate that they want diagnoses framed in a positive way should have their request honored.[6] Values of loyalty, integrity, solidarity, and compassion must enter into decisions about what to tell patients who have different cultural expectations from those of the predominant Western society in which they live.[7]

Finally, patients and families who wish to know about their current situation in order to prepare and to plan for the future need to be given full and accurate information. Many persons recognize that the pervasive denial of death discussed in chapter 1 is unrealistic and untenable; they accept that we should prepare for death well in advance. Such preparation may include taking account of our lives, spiritual repentance and prayer, seeing old friends for a last time, reconciling with those from whom we have been estranged, and making a will or otherwise getting our legal affairs in order. All such preparations for death are an important part of the process of healing, of reclaiming our wholeness. Too many of these preparations may be left undone if persons do not realize and acknowledge that the end is near. Thus, the responsibilities of truthful communication are also founded on the need to allow those who are gravely ill to prepare for death.

DEVELOPING ADVANCE DIRECTIVES FOR THE USE OF
LIFE-SUSTAINING TREATMENT

We applaud the desire of a growing number of people to plan ahead for a time of critical illness and to tell others what they want done if their condition cannot be reversed or its reversal would be very burdensome. Preparation for death was urged by the Anglican divine, Jeremy Taylor, who observed, "And how, if you were to die yourself? You know you must. Only be ready for it by the preparation of a good life, and then it is the greatest good that ever happened to thee."[8] Engaging in advance planning for the end of life is part of what it means today to live faithfully.

It is appropriate for Christians to take steps to try to ensure that their lives will not be extended by medical means beyond their time in pain and indignity. Many realize that being prepared to receive certain sorts of medical treatments and not others near the end of life can allow them to live more fully and comfortably in their remaining days. They also recognize that such preparation avoids leaving those they love in a state of uncertainty, vexation, and worry because they lack information about what sort of care to provide at this crucial time. Families are greatly helped by a clear and formal statement of a loved one's wishes about end-of-life care made in advance of critical illness that may lead to death.

There are many ways, both written and spoken, in which we can let our professional caregivers, family, and friends know what sort of care we want when we are approaching death. The best method—and the one that all states recognize legally—is the use of formal *advance directives*. These are written documents or verbal instructions that allow people to state their preferences about future treatment when they become unable to make decisions because of critical illness or imminent death. Advance directives enable them to anticipate difficulties in their medical care that might arise near the end of life and to indicate how they want to have these addressed.[9]

One form of advance directive is the *treatment directive*, usually known as the *living will*. By using this sort of directive, a person can specify in writing (1) those treatments that he or she definitely wants or wishes to refuse near the end of life and (2) the conditions for which he or she does or does not want such treatment at that time. Living wills were originally recognized legally only for those who were thought to be terminally ill. Today, in some states, they also cover the situation in which persons are in a persistent vegetative state with no hope of recovery. These treatment directives are understood to be a legitimate element in good end-of-life decision making for all patients, and in all conditions. Physicians and family members are on sound legal and ethical ground when their decisions are guided by the prior treatment directives of patients who can no longer speak for themselves. Such directives are most effective when those who write them give copies to their physicians, clergypersons, and families, and, most important, when they talk about these documents with these people.

Although many states have specified language that they require or recommend for living wills, most states will recognize documents that do not precisely match that language—as long as the document indicates clearly what sort of treatment the author wants and does not want. Indeed, most states also honor clear oral statements about future treatment decisions made by a competent person, even after that person has lost decision-making capacity.

Experience with living wills over the last two decades suggests that they have some limitations as a way of responding to the problems of dying. First, it is often impossible for a person writing a living will to anticipate the specific medical conditions and treatment options that may arise near the end of his or her life. Thus, use of this instrument cannot preclude the exercise of judgment by healthcare professionals and families in particular circumstances. Living wills that give vague statements, such as "no heroic measures," are not helpful. On the other hand, if statements in living wills are too specific, for instance, "no surgery," family members will be left to wonder what to do in situations when surgery might have a palliative effect on the person they love and make his or her end more comfortable.

Second, some families are concerned that a member who has written a living will has changed gradually over time and now has different needs and wishes near the end of life from those he or she anticipated earlier in a treatment directive. In some instances, a person experiencing dementia seems to become a very different person. As a consequence, family and friends may wonder whether to honor the wishes that he or she expressed earlier in a living will, since they no longer appear to apply to this seemingly new person.

Third, as a practical matter, living wills are often not operative parts of a patient's medical record. They may be physically separate from the patient, forgotten by all and sundry, or simply not included in the patient's chart. And, even if they are known, they may be overridden by a convincing family member who, for reasons good or bad, disagrees with the terms specified in the will and expresses this disagreement firmly and consistently.

These limitations of living wills should not lead us to conclude that they are valueless. Even if a living will is vague, it will give some evidence of the person's wishes and beliefs, and that type of guidance is always pertinent to end-of-life decisions. Because individuals and their values do change over time, it is important for those who have made out living wills to review them periodically and make sure that their treatment directives still express their deepest wishes and values. The concern, however, that a person with dementia is no longer the same person, and that his or her living will therefore is no longer valid, seems misguided. Although those with dementia do undergo great changes, they remain the same persons. They retain a sense of personal identity and continue to reflect cherished lifelong values until they reach the very last stages of this illness. Out of respect for them and these values, it is appropriate to allow the wishes they expressed earlier in a treatment directive to govern their care near the end of life unless these clearly do not fit the current situation.

In summary, the living will can be invaluable to family and physicians as a general statement of the hope, fears, and expectations of a person. It can give others a benchmark for making decisions about the care of a no-longer-competent person. Although a living will cannot provide an iron-clad guarantee that its author's choices will be honored in every detail, this sort of advance directive is morally important as an expression of a person's deepest values. Moreover, it can be an invaluable psychological aid to families and friends who struggle with treatment decisions for a loved one who can no longer communicate preferences. Indeed, family and caring professionals may come to view the living will as a gift to them from the dying person.

Yet, as valuable as a living will is, it may not be enough to have this one kind of advance directive to ensure that a person's values and goals will be respected near the end of life. Typically, it is advantageous to have an agent or a proxy to speak for the patient when a living will is unclear or ineffective or when unanticipated circumstances arise. To designate such an agent or proxy, individuals can use the other form of advance directive available for this purpose, the durable power of attorney for health care.

The durable power of attorney for health care is a legal instrument that enables persons to specify who shall make healthcare decisions for them when they cannot decide for themselves. It applies not just when they are terminally ill or in a persistent vegetative state, as is the case for living wills, but no matter what the condition of the author. It holds in force when someone is unable to decide for him- or herself—and only then. If someone who once lost decision-making power regains it, that person once again resumes making treatment decisions. In the forms in which it appears in many states, the durable power of attorney also allows its author to add to it instructions to his or her agent. Thus, although one may choose to have both a durable power of attorney and a living will, *if* a person chooses to develop *only one* of these advance directives, the durable power of attorney for health care is preferable. This is because it covers both treatment decisions and who should make them on behalf of the author.

When a person designates a healthcare agent in a durable power of attorney and later loses decision-making capacity, that agent is empowered to act on that person's behalf and to make binding decisions for him or her. That friend or family member's choices should be respected so long as the patient remains unable to decide for him- or herself. The agent is required to make the decision in the way that the person who appointed him or her would have made it. This is known as the "substituted judgment" standard, meaning that the agent substitutes the judgment of the incapacitated person for his or her own. When an agent does not know what the person would have chosen, he or she is to choose in light of what would promote the patient's good. This is known as the "best interests" standard. It requires the agent to set aside his or her interests and to make primary those of the person who has appointed him or her.

As is the case with living wills, the durable power of attorney has some limitations. First, it is often impossible for the agent to know what the author of the advance directive would want done in a specific situation. They may not have spoken about it together before the person lost decision-making capacity, and the agent may not be sure of what would be most conducive to that person's good at this point in time. Thus, neither the living will nor the durable power of attorney precludes the exercise of judgment by others in particular circumstances.

Second, it is as true of a durable power of attorney for health care as it is of a living will that the person who wrote the document may have changed gradually over time. After becoming unable to make treatment decisions, that person may have different needs and wishes from those he or she had expressed in an advance directive earlier. This can leave the agent in a quandary about whether to honor the earlier choices conveyed by the author of the durable power of attorney or whether to modify them in light of current circumstances.

Finally, the durable power of attorney requires its author to place exceptional trust in one individual to care for him or her faithfully. It calls upon the appointed agent to set aside his or her own interests when they do not mesh with those of the patient and to honor the Anglican understanding of right relationships. This is a great deal to expect and risks allowing the agent, inadvertently or intentionally, to disregard the patient's good.

Yet these difficulties are not fatal to the durable power of attorney form of advance directive. Durable powers of attorney, as is the case for all advance directives, revolve around matters of good faith, good will, and good judgment. The risks associated with the use of this instrument reveal that it is essential for those appointing an agent to select someone with these virtues. In most cases, the agent will make the well being and self-determination of the patient primary, responding in ways that are in keeping with the values and beliefs that they share or that are unique to the patient. In the rare case in which this is not the case, family, friends, and professional caregivers can step in to guard against harm to and to support the patient's welfare.

The durable power of attorney form of advance directive is based on an assumption that we are responsible for each other. This reflects the Anglican conviction that Christian faith is corporate and that we are inextricably embedded in community. At the same time, it realistically anticipates the possibility of disagreement among family members and other concerned persons as death draws near. Indeed, both living wills and durable powers of attorney point to the need of the individual for the larger presence, love, support, and prayers of the community. The development of advance directives represents more than filling out written forms. These directives promote planning, communication, and interaction and represent a concrete response to the Anglican call to accept the reality and inevitability of death. For all of these reasons, we reiterate the call of the Seventieth General Convention of the Episcopal Church for members to execute advance directives "during good health and competence, [for] the execution of such advance written directives constitute loving and moral acts."[10]

CARING FOR THOSE WITH LIMITED DECISION-MAKING CAPACITY WHO ARE APPROACHING DEATH

We must recognize that some adults have never had the capacity to make their own treatment decisions or have had this capacity only intermittently. And most children have not yet developed to a point at which they can make their own choices about treatment near the end of life. These persons raise an even harder set of questions about decision making near the end of life. Such questions should be resolved by considering the individual's good, needs, and purposes, broadly defined. When we say "broadly defined," we mean to suggest once again that the good of persons is not to be defined exclusively in terms of extended life.

Those who are approaching death, including those who have been decisionally incapacitated much or all of their lives, have many needs and purposes besides that of living long. They have a concern about their self-presentation to others, about reconciliation with those with whom they may have been estranged, about comfort and peace. These should also be weighed into the choice of treatment for them. An incompetent person's interests should not automatically be identified with maximal duration of life. A long life is cause for celebration; all other things being equal, the more life the better, as we have maintained in chapter 3. But today it is possible to deform dying and to torment persons as they die, particularly those who cannot fend for themselves and make their own choices.

There is no Christian obligation to initiate or continue medical treatment that discomforts or is disrespectful to those near death who lack decision-making capacity. Their condition does not put them outside the pale of human care or outside the call to recognize that their good as human beings has many facets that should be taken into consideration as decisions are made for them. Moreover, they should be included in decisions about their care to the extent that their cognitive capacities allow. Our conviction that we are responsible for one another and are drawn together in community as members of the body of Christ means that we must care for those who are vulnerable and cannot make treatment decisions for themselves in ways that respect and promote their good and their concerns.

Children represent a special case of those who have limited decision-making capacity. Infants and very young children cannot generally be considered capable of participating in decisions on their behalf. As children mature, however, their wishes can carry increasing weight in the decision-making process. Many adolescents, well before they reach the age of legal majority, are able to make thoughtful and fitting decisions about their care and their future. Although children of any age are not legally allowed to give *consent* for their medical treatment (or to refuse it), most physicians and medical ethicists recognize the importance of seeking the *assent* of a sufficiently mature child to decisions directly affecting his or her health, physical integrity, or possible death.

Parents are recognized as the persons responsible for choices regarding the lives of their children because of the love that binds them to their children and because they have a history of life together in which they have shared values, joys, and sorrows. When the choices are of the sort we are discussing in this book—decisions in which parents must choose between the certainty of death for their child and a faint hope of extended life accompanied by suffering—their parental responsibility may be almost unbearable.

One of the most difficult aspects of end-of-life decision making on a child's behalf is what seems to be its "unnaturalness." Virtually every other facet of parenting, including the obligation to protect the child from physical or emotional harm, is focused on the continued, maturing life of the child. There is the firm expectation that he or she will both outlive the parents and, in time, add more descendants to the ongoing family line. End-of-life decisions bring into inescapable conflict the need of parents to protect their children from fruitless pain and suffering and their equally compelling need to have their children live and thrive. This distressing and poignant conflict is also experienced by others—family, friends, fellow parishioners, healthcare professionals—engaged in caring for and about the children. The Anglican moral vision of the interdependence of human good with right relationships and the responsible use of power is especially relevant in these situations.

The Church's ministry is crucial for parents facing such a trial. The Christian tradition counters the human fear of early death—often expressed as dying before one has lived a "full" life—with the assurance of resurrection. Likewise, Christians trust that, as adults, our true destiny is still to be found in the hands and heart of God, rather than simply in the continuity of our lineage.

Nevertheless, the parents of a dying child must face the remainder of their temporal existence without their beloved child and without fulfillment of the joyful expectations that surrounded that child's life and future. The enormity of this loss—for the family *and* for the community—should not be underestimated, nor can the lonely weight of parental responsibility in making such intolerable choices. Ongoing close sustenance by a community of prayer and presence is essential. In the face of a child's dying, our Christian reliance on a transcendent hope becomes critically important for continued faithful living. The faithful, healing community embodies that hope as it surrounds and supports the parents and family through their decisions and their grief.

In this chapter, we have addressed our responsibility to use our freedom to make choices near the end of life in ways that serve human good—our own and that of others. Faithful living calls on us to be sensitive and responsive to the theological and ethical understandings and attitudes that are at the core of practical piety and to make decisions near the end of life in light of these. Our call to live out God's purposes in the world means that we need to overcome our denial of death. Doing so gives us an opportunity to prepare for it in advance and to make responsible treatment choices when we are at its door.

Although advances in medical technology and the development of new treatment modalities raise new questions and new choices for us today, the Christian faith and the Anglican tradition, in particular, have certain significant resources with which to respond to them. Among these is a distinctively Anglican set of attitudes toward death and dying and a variety of ways of responding to those in need and despair that has informed our discussion all along. We turn in the next chapter to an exploration of these attitudes, virtues, and ways of responding as they infuse the life of the congregation.

---

1. *The Official Report of the Lambeth Conference, 1998,* "Called to Full Humanity. Section 1 Report. Theme 5: Euthanasia," (Harrisburg, Pa.: Morehouse, 1999), 101–106, 102.

2. See point 5 of the resolution, "Establish Principles with Regard to the Prolongation of Life," of the Seventieth General Convention of 1991, reprinted in Committee on Medical Ethics, Episcopal Diocese of Washington, *Toward a Good Christian Death: Crucial Treatment Choices* (Harrisburg, Pa.: Morehouse, 1999), 127.

3. Committee on Medical Ethics, Episcopal Diocese of Washington, *Toward a Good Christian Death,* 15–16.

4. Lawrence O. Gostin, "Informed Consent, Cultural Sensitivity, and Respect for Persons," *Journal of the American Medical Association,* vol. 274, No. 10, 1995, 844–845.

5. Leslie J. Blackhall, Sheila T. Murphy, Gelya Frank, Vicki Michel, and Stanley Azen, "Ethnicity and Attitudes toward Patient Autonomy," *Journal of the American Medical Association,* vol. 274, No. 10, 1995, 820–825.

6. Joseph A. Carrese, and Lorna A. Rhodes, "Western Bioethics on the Navajo Reservation," *Journal of the American Medical Association,* vol. 274, No. 10, 1995, 826–829.

7. Thomas H. Murray, "Communities Need More than Autonomy," *Hastings Center Report,* vol. 24, No. 3, 1994, 32–33.

8. Jeremy Taylor, *Holy Living and Holy Dying,* 2 vols., ed. P. G. Stanwood (London: Clarendon, 1989), vol. 1, 3.

9. Committee on Medical Ethics, Episcopal Diocese of Washington, *Before You Need Them: Advance Directives for Health Care, Living Wills and Durable Powers of Attorney* (Cincinnati, Ohio: Forward Movement, 1995).

10. See point 7 of the resolution, "Establish Principles with Regard to the Prolongation of Life," of the Seventieth General Convention of 1991, reprinted in Committee on Medical Ethics, Episcopal Diocese of Washington, *Toward a Good Christian Death,* 128.

CHAPTER 6

ACCEPTING, CARING, AND MOURNING

Engaging the difficult ethical issues discussed in the previous two chapters requires us to sustain a distinctive moral perspective toward faithful living and faithful dying. That is difficult to do on our own. Therefore, in this chapter we turn to three attitudes that we need to nourish within our congregations if we are to deal honestly and constructively with death and dying. They relate to remembering that we are mortal, sustaining a community of care, and comforting those who are bereaved—that is, accepting, caring, and mourning.

Our conviction that God is incarnate expresses the Christian faith that God is present in the midst of our daily life. Thus, we are called to meet God in the ordinary day-by-day activities of acknowledging that we are mortal, caring for those who are dying, and mourning with those who mourn. The congregations that form the heart of the Episcopal Church have a significant role to play in supporting us as individuals and as communities in carrying out these activities. Local parishes are the primary locus of Christian teaching and the formation of conscience within the Church. They are the force that forms us as moral agents. Moreover, in acting as accepting, caring, and mourning people, congregations also act as healing communities. While certain members are called specifically to work in the healing professions—as nurses, therapists, or physicians, for example—all members are asked to participate in God's healing ministry through our prayers, acts of mercy, and faithful presence with those who are ill and those who care for them.

ACCEPTING OUR MORTALITY

Sustaining an honest attitude toward death while living in hope is not easy. Anxiety, exhaustion, distraction, disappointment, a series of senseless reverses or even honest appraisal of our prospects may drive us to denial or cynicism. Forming ourselves to live with the hope and sufferings of daily existence and with the shadow of death that hangs over them requires work. Congregations, as essential elements of the living church, must be unafraid to address the questions raised near the end of life. As William F. May points out:

> The Lord of the church is not ruler of a surface kingdom. His dominion is nothing if it does not go at least six feet deep. The church affirms the one Lord who went down into the grave, fought a battle with the power of death, and by his own death brought death to an end. For this reason, the church must be unafraid to speak of death. It is compelled to speak of death as the servant of Jesus Christ, the Crucified and Risen Savior, who has freed men from the power of the Unmentionable One.[1]

Congregational efforts can help us to cut through our denial of death and realistically engender hope among us. Speaking of death honestly, however, seems to be a lesson that every parish, priest, and parishioner must relearn. It is a corporate or collective task that requires courage and sensitivity within local church communities.

There are fairly specific ways in which members of congregations can uphold each other as we overcome our socially sanctioned denial of death. When the community gathers in common worship, clergy can seize this opportunity directly and openly to explore the subject of our dying in preaching. Not only in sermons but also in homilies on various occasions, they can find a place to refer to the inevitability of death and the hope for life eternal. Some priests avoid references to dying and death in their sermons out of concern that those listening will find the topic disturbing and unsettling. Yet such references can offer joy and comfort, rather than gloom and doom, when they emphasize that Jesus, who knew death in all its dimensions, exposed its powerlessness against the love of God. In these sermons and homilies, as well as in the course of pastoral care, ministers can remind parishioners that *The Book of Common Prayer* offers powerful prayers to nurture them in the face of death. The four "Prayers for Use by a Sick Person" (BCP, 461) can be especially helpful to Christians as they ask with trust that God's presence may sustain them as they struggle with illness. One of these prayers recognizes that even weakened persons can serve God. Thus, we read:

> This is another day, O Lord. I know not what it will bring forth, but make me ready, Lord, for whatever it may be. If I am to stand up, help me to stand bravely. If I am to sit still, help me to sit quietly. If I am to lie low, help me to do it patiently. And if I am to do nothing, let me do it gallantly. Make these words more than words, and give me the Spirit of Jesus.

Congregations can also grapple with our unwillingness to face up to the inevitability of death by providing intentional education. Some congregations report that they have had great success at raising their members' awareness of the need to prepare for dying with a series of educational talks and discussions at adult forums during Lent or other appropriate seasons of the church year. In such discussions, they have drawn upon the experience of health professionals, ethicists, attorneys, funeral directors, and others within the community to overcome a general reluctance to bring the subject of dying into the light. Some parishes have found it useful to view and explore such videos as one from the Diocese of Colorado, "Before Death Happens,"[2] which provides information about planning ahead through wills and advance directives, as well as about making practical choices. The books by the Committee on Medical Ethics of the Diocese of Washington, *Before You Need Them*[3] and *Assisted Suicide and Euthanasia,*[4] have been used by many congregations in adult forums and study groups. The former explains the use of advance directives for health care in a useful question-and-answer format and the latter provides a wide-ranging discussion of whether it is ever morally right actively to end the lives of the dying. A new book, *Toward a Good Christian Death: Crucial Treatment Choices*[5] by the Committee on Medical Ethics of the Diocese of Washington is also designed for use by parish discussion groups, as well as other groups and individuals concerned about making difficult treatment choices near life's end. Forward Movement Publications has a wealth of booklets directed toward end-of-life matters that can be recommended to parishioners at adult education gatherings.[6]

In an interesting new turn, Episcopal churches around the country are creating a new *ars moriendi,* or "art of dying," literature. In medieval and early modern times, books were written to help people prepare for dying. These books provided shared norms on how to die and how to mourn, and they applied to all, king and slave alike. Today, individual congregations and groups of them are developing a similar sort of literature. They are writing booklets, pamphlets, forms, hand-outs, and other materials about matters that arise near the end of life that are of special concern to parishioners today. The End of Life Task Force has received a wealth of such resources from parochial clergy and laypersons. Their names and locations can be found in the acknowledgment section at the beginning of this book. These materials are designed not only to bring Anglican theology and practices to the aid of those who face dying and those close to them, but also to provide practical information and advice for those attending to the myriad details that surround dying and death.

For example, one booklet, *Last Things: A Parish Resource for the Time of Death,* covers such matters as grief, a Christian perspective on death, planning for death, burial practices, the rites of burial, and stewardship in death. It was initially developed by St. Thomas Episcopal Church in Cincinnati, Ohio, and then began to circulate among other congregations in the diocese of Southern Ohio. It has since moved far and wide, and has been adapted for their own unique use by congregations in Pennsylvania,

Wisconsin, and elsewhere. The End of Life Task Force presents a recent version of *Last Things* from one of these churches, St. Matthias Episcopal Church in Waukesha, Wisconsin, in the appendix to this book.

Other pamphlets, brochures, and leaflets related to death and dying that we have received from churches around the country focus on one or two topics, such as providing assistance to those planning funerals, executing wills, developing advance directives, coping when a family member dies, and hospice care. Some of these materials are beginning to appear on church web sites to assist not only parishioners but also others in the community who are searching for help with these matters. Through this contemporary "art of dying" literature, the conspiracy of silence about death is being broken within the congregations of the Episcopal Church so that their members and those close to them can find care and support when death arrives.

SUSTAINING A COMMUNITY OF CARE

Facing death can be a devastating experience in which a large part of one's world is lost. Those who are dying grieve for the impending end of their own lives and the prospect of having to let go of those they love. Dying alone can emphasize that loss. In our culture, people's lives can end in physical and social contexts that are remote from the places, persons, and communities that have situated them. Such isolated dying results from our social mobility, our success in treating accidents and infectious diseases, and our ability to provide highly specialized medical competencies and institutions. Many fear this will be their fate. Indeed, the fear of abandonment can be worse than that of dying or death itself.

An isolated death severs us from important relationships, from our ability to participate in the communities that have defined us as the persons we are. This is why the Prayer Book envisions death as a community event rather than an individual incident in our biological trajectory. This is revealed in the service of "Ministration at the Time of Death," which indicates that "when possible, it is desirable that members of the family and friends come together to join in the Litany" (BCP, 462). This service embodies the Christian vision of each person as a significant member of the community, a part of God's human creation, set within the body of Christ, which is the Church. Furthermore, the "Prayers for the Sick" (BCP, 458–460) provide resources for all of us when one of us is dying. They assume that others who share our common life in the Church will care for us and pray with us as our illness becomes progressively more serious and death appears on the horizon.

Again, Anglicanism maintains that humans are social at root, that Christian faith is corporate, and that we are interdependent creatures.

Consequently, we have a duty to sustain—and, if necessary, to create—communities of care for each other and to be open, present, and attentive to one another near the end of life.

Those who accept the reality that they are dying must go on to grapple with many other concerns. Some struggle with the nagging belief that their illness is somehow deserved or a judgment against them for a specific act of wrongdoing. In countering such convictions, some clergy have found it helpful to explore with parishioners in sermons and in classes the service of "Ministration to the Sick" in *The Book of Common Prayer* (BCP, 453). This service reflects the church's theological response to those who are ill and near death. In this, it provides a change in emphasis from earlier Prayer Books, for it no longer expresses resignation to a deserved illness or death, but puts its stress on healing. Moreover, it asks not only for bodily healing but also for healing of the whole person.[7] A separate section, "Ministration at the Time of Death" (BCP, 462), acknowledges that some people will not recover from their illnesses and speaks openly of death. Here, ministers can point out to their flock, Christians will find prayers holding the promise of redemption, pardon, rest, and refreshment. These prayers and liturgies set an open and balanced tone that clergy can appropriate to help members of their congregation address their fears and questions about dying.

As this discussion suggests, another important form of care for those coping with concerns about dying is spontaneous private or extemporaneous petitionary prayer. This sort of prayer, so much a part of the life of serious Christians, naturally becomes more frequent as illness becomes more severe. Questions arise at times about what should and should not be included in such prayers. Family members, parishioners, and even patients themselves who become impatient with drawn-out suffering ask whether prayer for death is acceptable in such difficult circumstances. When this question arises, it is a matter of Christian responsibility to ensure that the circumstances are no more dire than they need to be—that adequate care has been provided for pain, discomfort, depression, and spiritual torment. An expressed desire by a patient to die may be a signal that forms of care should be adjusted.

But that said, things cannot always be made as easy as we would like, and sometimes it is only natural to hope and to pray that the ordeal end. The task force believes it is important to distinguish a prayer for the release from suffering from a prayer for death. "Let him go" or "Take her" seem more appropriate and theologically preferable to "Make it stop" or "Enough; let him die." But, when all is said and done, honesty is the most important virtue in prayer and this is not the time to be overly concerned with the exact verbal formulations that come to people's minds and lips. God's will be done; we can try our best to care well and to comfort the afflicted.

The congregation as a community can participate in caring for those who face death in a variety of ways. With the revival of the healing ministry in recent years, many parishes now offer a healing service. This ministry provides an opportunity for clergy and lay ministers to say something about the Anglican understanding of healing versus curing and about the healing of the whole person that can surround faithful dying. Anecdotal reports that the task force has received from clergy and parishioners indicate that a reluctance to ask God for healing of those who are dying that has characterized Episcopal congregations in the past is receding. Thus, the introduction of this form of ministry into parishes and missions can help to meet some of the special needs of those who are approaching death.

Healing services can take many forms. In some Episcopal churches, those who seek healing during the Eucharist are asked to come forward to the altar rail or to a side area that is more private to be prayed with and, sometimes, anointed by a priest or by lay ministers. At other churches, those receiving communion who seek healing may stay at the rail when others leave. At still other churches, there is a short and separate healing service immediately after the Eucharist, using prayers from *The Book of Common Prayer* or from a "A Public Service of Healing" in *The Book of Occasional Services* (pages 162–169).[8] In all of these forms, the healing service can bring a "life-giving, life-mending experience"[9] to those with a variety of needs and concerns, including those who are nearing death.

Visitation of the sick provides another important dimension of congregational care and a significant way in which Christians can learn to speak of death openly. Such visitation is a practice that emerges from Anglican convictions about community and fellowship in the face of separation and death. This ministry need not be restricted to clergy but also can be carried out by laypersons, many of whom have a gift for offering spiritual companionship to those who are seriously ill. In providing support and guidance to those who face death, clerical and congregational visitors can themselves rediscover an honest fear of death and a firm faith in resurrection. Such programs of visitation are sometimes included within a larger program of health ministry that congregations have developed to meet their unique needs and to express the special gifts of those within them.

Congregational health ministries take a variety of forms. Some focus on the health of individuals, while others emphasize the health of groups within the congregation or of the whole community surrounding it. The National Episcopal Health Ministries provides information and resources to congregations to assist them in establishing their own healthcare ministries. The program was organized to help the church at the local level "to live out Jesus' command to heal and to make whole in body, mind, and spirit."

Churches with this form of ministry call upon nurses, clergy, hospital chaplains, social workers, teachers, health educators, and others in the congregation who are committed to the health of the whole person to put it into action. A congregational health ministry can take many forms, depending on the needs of the specific church. It can include programs focused on dimensions of dying, such as seminars on end-of-life matters, respite care for those tending to the sick and dying, and/or support groups for those who are grieving. The National Episcopal Health Ministries has several valuable printed resources designed to assist congregations that are just starting to develop a health ministry.[10] For further information about this program, contact National Episcopal Health Ministries, St. Paul's Episcopal Church, 10 West 61 Street, Indianapolis, Indiana 46208. The telephone number is (317) 253-1277.

Parish nurses often lead health-ministry programs in Episcopal congregations around the country. These programs emphasize prevention of illness, healthcare education, and attention to a range of health concerns, bringing spiritual sensitivity and healing to this ministry. Parish nurses serve as counselors, referral resources, and patient advocates to whom members of the congregation may come to talk about such matters as their diet, medication, blood pressure, and worries. This program can be immensely helpful to those with chronic conditions who are moving toward death and who need assistance with simple health problems but do not require acute medical assistance. Parish nurses are registered nurses who have been educated through the endorsed curriculum of the International Parish Nurse Resource Center. This program is offered to Episcopalians through a partnership between National Episcopal Health Ministries and the Seabury Institute of Seabury-Western Seminary in Evanston, Illinois. Further information about parish nursing is available from the International Parish Nurse Resource Center, 205 West Touhy Avenue, Suite 124, Park Ridge, Illinois 60068 at telephone number (800) 556-5368 or from the National Episcopal Health Ministries cited above.

Stephen Ministries is another program devoted to helping congregations to care for those who suffer and those who are in crisis, including those who are approaching death. It provides training at a central location for those within parishes who are drawn to help others within their congregations and communities who are facing difficult pastoral situations. This form of ministry emphasizes four components: training small-group leaders in practical skills, providing a method of supervision and support for use with these leaders, offering organizational and administrative resources, and equipping those in the congregation who will set up and maintain the entire system. Stephen Ministries can be reached at 2045

Innerbelt Business Center Drive, St. Louis, Missouri 63114-5765 for further information. Its telephone number is (314) 428-2600.

Other programs that may be of assistance to those who are dying and those caring for them include such ministries as local Samaritan Societies,[11] Befrienders, and Call to Care. These offer various types of assistance, such as crisis care, care of the chronically ill, and supportive care for families of the ill and dying.

The involvement of many Episcopal congregations with local hospices that care for the dying is a cause for rejoicing. (See the earlier discussion of hospice in chapter 4.) These congregations have organized parish volunteers who serve on hospice teams that also include healthcare workers from several disciplines. Their goals are to provide integrated hospice care to those who are dying and their families and to help them develop effective coping strategies during the process of dying. Congregations with such programs find that they create greater awareness of the existence of hospice among their members and that this, in turn, leads members to make more effective use of this form of care when it is their time to die. The End of Life Task Force urges other congregations to respond to the call to care for those near death and to explore the possibility of working with hospice services.

It is also important for congregations to remember that many of the needs for care experienced by those near the end of life, within hospice programs and without, are not at all esoteric, but quite mundane. Meals must be prepared, houses cleaned, errands run, bills paid. People need rides, often at short notice; family caregivers need respite care. A recent study of assistance provided to those who are terminally ill and their families indicates that few receive assistance from volunteers.[12] Members of congregations should be willing and able to provide some of this help as part of their daily responsibilities as Christians. Furthermore, they need to be sensitive to their responsibilities as citizens in assuring that we have public policies in place that will extend hospice care to all in the United States who are approaching death within the foreseeable future and are in need of such support.

It is not only those near the end of life and their families who need care and support from within the congregation. The task force wants to stress the importance of providing pastoral support, education, and a listening ear for health caregivers—nurses, physicians, social workers, technicians, paramedics, administrative staff, and others—as they struggle to make compassionate care for the dying a reality across our country.[13] Attention should be paid to developing special forms of ministry helpful to these healthcare workers, opening up ways in which their experience and that of those who are ill or bereaved can be channeled back into the life of the parish. Indeed, the Episcopal Church as a whole can support their efforts to make care for the dying more attentive and responsive by offering them prayer and counsel. If the Church fails in this responsibility, it can scarcely claim credibility when it attempts to preach about such matters as physician-assisted suicide.

Although clergy will play a leading role in these initiatives, it is important to remember that clergy also require ministering. They, too, need support in attempting to overcome their own drive to deny the reality of death and their sense of powerlessness before it. The dedication of the community is required to keep the conviction of God's love and sovereignty alive for those who minister to parishioners near death and to those who love them. The Church must not absent itself from its pastoral call to listen to clergy who express a need for greater support or from its responsibility to provide them with sustenance for the stresses with which they live as they carry out their ministry.

COMFORTING THE BEREAVED

Our hope in the resurrection expresses our conviction that death is not the last word. God does not abandon us to death. At the same time, the resurrection is not a matter of saving us from this life. God is incarnate, enfleshed in our daily lives. The death of another is therefore reason for grief and mourning. As the note about the liturgy for the dead in *The Book of Common Prayer* indicates, although we rejoice in the certainty that we, too, shall be raised:

> This joy, however, does not make human grief unchristian. The very love we have for each other in Christ brings deep sorrow when we are parted by death. Jesus himself wept at the grave of his friend. So, while we rejoice that one we love has entered into the nearer presence of our Lord, we sorrow in sympathy with those who mourn. (BCP, 507)

Grief, tears, the dull ache of missing and loneliness, are natural and appropriate responses to death. A final need for communities is to care for those who mourn. Thus, ministry to those who are bereaved is an essential component of our congregational attention to the dying.

The Christian affirmation that death is not the final word and that nothing, not even death, can separate us from God's love can provide great comfort and perspective to those who are mourning the loss of someone they have loved dearly. An especially treasured prayer that offers care and support to those who are grieving can be found in *The Book of Common Prayer*:

> O merciful Father, who hast taught us in thy holy Word that thou dost not willingly afflict or grieve the children of men: Look with pity upon the sorrows of thy servant for whom our prayers are offered. Remember *him*, O

Lord, in mercy, nourish *his* soul with patience, comfort *him* with a sense of thy goodness, lift up thy countenance upon *him*, and give *him* peace; through Jesus Christ our Lord. (BCP, 831)

The very acts asked of God in this prayer—"look with pity . . . remember . . . nourish his soul . . . comfort . . . give peace"—can become the acts of Christian congregations in which there are persons who grieve. Yet these are acts that members of congregations, who are surrounded by a death-denying culture, often find difficult to perform.

"Look with pity," instead of looking the other way, the prayer reminds us. The isolation that individuals and families of the dying feel during an illness is often accentuated following death. The immediate outpouring of sympathy and comfort at the time of death and at burial services frequently is followed by a deafening silence. People are reluctant to call or to visit for fear of intrusion. Individuals may also resist visiting out of fear that they might say the wrong thing and thereby add to grief. The Christian congregation has a responsibility to "look with pity," to look in on and to be present to those who are learning to live with loss.

"Remember," instead of avoiding talking about the dead person in the presence of the living. One of the most frequent complaints of those who grieve is that congregational visitors are reluctant to use the name of the deceased. Not wanting to add to the pain of those who mourn, they avoid any mention of the beloved individual. The community of faith, however, is a remembering community, one that recalls its faithful in prayer and its loved members who have died in daily conversation. Death is a reality to be shared, not shunned, within our community. Christians, who are confident of God's presence to those they love who have died, can help one another to cope with grief by continuing to remember those persons by name.

"Nourish" brings to mind that in many places it is customary to bring food into a household that has suffered a loss. The Christian congregation nourishes those who grieve by bringing itself. It does so not only through visits from clergy and laypersons, but also by means of grief support groups. Congregations can also assist in the long-term grieving process. A pamphlet created by the Good Grief Group of St. Mark's-in-the-Valley Episcopal Church in Los Olivos, California,[14] explains to those who are newly bereaved that their sorrow will not necessarily disappear after a certain length of time. It advises them that:

> Grieving the loss of your loved one is a fact of life from which there is no recovering. You learn to live with it, cope with it and survive it. The tears will abate, the anger soften and the future will be brighter than today. But you will not be cured. To some extent, there will always be a hole. Yet in time, if you allow this hole to exist, the pain will lessen and you will feel good that you conscientiously allowed this space.

To meet the needs of those who are bereaved, congregations can arrange to make periodic visits over a long period of time, much as some hospitals and hospices have regular contacts with families after a death at certain intervals—six weeks, three months, six months, and then annually. These long-term regular visits open the door for those who still grieve to express themselves in ways they feel are still needed.

"Comfort" takes on a distinctive meaning at the time of grief. Frequently, the most comforting person to those who mourn is not necessarily the one who offers kind, religious thoughts and theologically correct answers but the person who is willing to listen. A grief shared, while perhaps not a grief relieved, can be a grief endured. The most comforting role of a church member, especially in the early stages of bereavement, might well be that of concerned listener rather than of religious truth teller. The person who is willing to be present and to listen is vital in the lives of those who newly mourn.

"Give peace," as in the Eucharist we share the peace. Although we are not the cause of God's peace, in sharing the peace we acknowledge it, name it, affirm it. We help one another to recognize the truth that when two or three are gathered together in Christ's name, his presence is known. The same is true when congregational visitors put aside fears and feelings of inadequacy and figuratively or literally dare to bring the kiss of peace into the household of those who grieve.

Some congregations have found it helpful to provide a memorial garden or columbarium on church grounds where the ashes of parishioners and their families may be buried. This follows an ancient Christian tradition in which the churchyard was the usual place for burial of the dead, offering a sense of connection between the living and those they love who have died. We provide two different sorts of information about memorial gardens or columbariums in the appendix. The pamphlet describing the Memorial Garden of Saint Andrew's Episcopal Church in Saratoga, California, presents the tradition, history, and procedures for the burial of ashes at that church. Creating such separate areas requires considerable planning and knowledge of state law. The regulations and conditions for the use of the columbarium at St. Peter's Church in Conway, Arkansas, which opened after two years of preparation, provide insight into the great care and details that must be taken into account in developing such a site. The resulting place of burial of ashes offers a site of comfort, spiritual strength, and tranquility to those who mourn.

Accepting death, caring for those who are dying, and reaching out to those who mourn are Christian attitudes that can uphold and support individuals and congregations as we shape our response to death. These attitudes can also inform the many decisions that confront us as we are dying or as we care for those near death. Congregations should nurture these attitudes and virtues in their individual members and in their common life together.

These attitudes are brought into the lives of those who face death within a healthcare system that has changed radically in recent years. The Church is called to respond to these changes not only through its congregations but also as a whole. In the next chapter, we ask two sets of questions. The first is: how should the Church as a body respond through its ordained and lay ministers to those making difficult treatment choices in the face of today's radically changed healthcare circumstances? The second is: what sort of expanded and new liturgies can the Church provide to support those who are near the end of life today and those close to them? We now turn to these questions.

---

1. William F. May, "The Sacral Power of Death in Contemporary Experience," in *On Moral Medicine: Theological Perspectives in Medical Ethics*, 2nd ed., ed. Stephen Lammers and Allen Verhey (Grand Rapids, Mich.: Eerdmans, 1998), 197–209.

2. "Before Death Happens" can be ordered from the Diocese of Colorado by contacting Video Sales, Episcopal Church Center, 1300 Washington St., Denver, Colorado 80203-2008. Their phone number is (303) 837-1173.

3. Committee on Medical Ethics, Episcopal Diocese of Washington, *Before You Need Them: Advance Directives for Health Care, Living Wills and Durable Powers of Attorney*," (Cincinnati, Ohio: Forward Movement Publications, 1995).

4. Committee on Medical Ethics, Episcopal Diocese of Washington, *Assisted Suicide and Euthanasia: Christian Moral Perspectives* (Harrisburg, Pa.: Morehouse Publishing, 1997).

5. Committee on Medical Ethics, Episcopal Diocese of Washington, *Toward a Good Christian Death: Crucial Treatment Choices* (Harrisburg, Pa.: Morehouse Publishing, 1999).

6. Forward Movement Publications, 412 Sycamore Street, Cincinnati, Ohio 45202.

7. Leonel L. Mitchell, *Praying Shapes Believing* (Harrisburg, Pa.: Morehouse, 1985), 207–216.

8. Avery Brooke, *Healing in the Landscape of Prayer* (Cambridge, Mass.: Cowley, 1996), 52–65.

9. The Episcopal Healing Ministry Foundation, *Report of the Joint Commission on the Ministry of Healing to the General Convention of the Episcopal Church, St. Louis Missouri, 1964, with Resolutions Adopted* (Cincinnati, 1987), 12.

10. Stephanie Ulrich, and Allen Brown, *Health Ministry in the Local Congregation*, and Jean Denton, *Steps to a Health Ministry in Your Episcopal Congregation*, both available through Rev. Jean Denton, R.N., National Episcopal Health Ministries, St. Paul's Church, 10 West 61 Street, Indianapolis, IN 46208.

11. For further information about a carefully organized local Samaritan Society, contact Rev. Loren Coyle, Trinity Episcopal Church, 2365 Pine Ave., Vero Beach, FL 32960-0528. His phone number is (561) 567-1146.

12. Ezekiel J. Emanuel, Diane L. Fairclough, Julia Slutsman, Hillel Alpert, DeWitt Baldwin, Linda L. Emanuel, "Assistance from Family Members, Friends, Paid Care Givers, and Volunteers in the Care of Terminally Ill Patients," *New England Journal of Medicine*, 1999, vol. 341, No. 13, 956–963.

13. See Margaret E. Mohrmann, *Medicine as Ministry: Reflections on Suffering, Ethics, and Hope* (Cleveland, Ohio: Pilgrim Press, 1995), 109–112.

14. To order, contact Rev. Charles H. Stacy, St. Mark's Church, P.O. Box 39, Los Olivos, CA 93441. His phone number is (805) 688-4454.

CHAPTER 7

ENRICHING THE CHURCH'S RESPONSE

The Anglican Communion has over the centuries nurtured a rich ministerial and liturgical tradition devoted to those who are dying. Today, as we find ourselves thrust into new social and healthcare realities, questions are being raised about whether the ministrations and rituals of the Church adequately meet the current needs and circumstances of those who learn that they will die. Does *The Book of Common Prayer* capture what faithful dying entails today, given the realities of eternally lit intensive care units, powerful new drugs, and advanced life-support systems? Do its liturgies and prayers address all-too-real nursing home scenarios of ever-changing attendants delivering medications on sterile carts, sing-along gatherings characterized by forced gaiety, and hallways haunted by the sighs and cries of those no longer aware of their surroundings? More broadly, is the Church doing justice to its baptismal call to "respect the dignity of every human being" as it seeks to "serve Christ in all persons" (BCP, 305), especially in those who are dying? How can the Church bring its distinctively Anglican theological and ethical understandings and its liturgies to help its ministers address the profound shifts that are taking place within the healthcare setting today?

While pastoral responses to persons who face death still include telling the story of how the Christian life is rooted in the community, grounded in worship, and upheld by prayer, there is growing concern about whether these traditional responses are sufficient. Comments that the End of Life Task Force has received from parochial priests, chaplains, and lay ministers reveal that a wide range of respondents feel they are striking out into uncharted areas when they assist those near death today. Often they do not feel adequately prepared for the journey and express a need for additional ministerial and liturgical signposts. They are seeking new educational resources and support as they uphold dying patients and their families in their attempts to cope with the terrible privacy imposed on them by an individualistic, death-denying culture. Moreover, ministers, ordained and lay alike, express a special interest in the creation of revised and expanded prayers and liturgies that they can bring to care for and comfort those near the end of life and those who surround them.

RESPONDING TO THE CONTEMPORARY REALITIES
OF MINISTERING TO THOSE NEAR DEATH

Anguished questions still spring up from those approaching death about the meaning of life, what ends are worth pursuing, how their illness fits into God's plan, whether they are up to faithful dying. These sorts of questions provide familiar terrain for ministers of the Church. Yet today's ministers are also being called to venture into new areas of ethical deliberation and care.[1] More specifically, they are being asked to respond to patients and families who ask how Christian commitments can shed light on whether they ought to use such technological realities as respirators and stomach feeding tubes to extend their lives as they near death. They are sought after for help in alleviating the pain of cancer, the dread of dementia, and, perhaps most of all, the fear of prolonged dying made possible by contemporary medical technology. They are expected to assist families bewildered about where to turn to find hospice care for a relative near death or whether to donate the organs of a family member who has died. In short, they are being called upon for new sorts of ethical, quasi-medical, and pastoral support by those near death who are attempting to preserve integrity and faith in the often isolating atmosphere of today's healthcare institutions.

At the same time, family structures at the nuclear and extended levels have become more fractured, and the circle of immediate friends and loved ones that used to surround people has become more geographically dispersed. As a result, ministers must consider a wider range of people than those within the classical family as they address the pastoral concerns of those near death. The vast distances over which families and friends have spread requires pastoral counselors to provide a series of ministrations to a variety of individuals who come and go in fluctuating patterns over extended periods of time. Thus, the Church needs to respond sensitively not only to dying persons but also to a variety of people surrounding them in light of the radically new dimensions in which we "live and move and have our being."

One priest who is a frequent hospital attendant depicts for the task force how poignant and difficult these new ethical and pastoral issues are.

> The call from the local hospital came from the emergency room nursing supervisor on a Saturday night. I was summoned to meet with a family that was very concerned about their mother, a member of the parish, who was being admitted with a massive coronary attack.

As soon as I arrived, I was immersed in a very stressful and sad family situation. The matriarch of the clan was dying, and family members were terribly upset about this sudden and traumatic event in their lives. I tried to offer whatever consolation I could and help them accept what seemed to be coming. As the evening wore on, it became apparent that her vital signs could not be sustained indefinitely on life-support systems. It was a painful and anguished realization for us all.

Finally, one of the doctors very carefully and with exquisite sensitivity asked the family whether the life-support systems should be removed. The family seemed to defer to me, seeking moral permission to "let her go peacefully." Slowly and reluctantly, we came to the conclusion that this was the right thing to do for her. I conducted a vigil for the rest of the night with the family, praying at the woman's bedside, and offered a final blessing as she died. I tried to be of comfort to the family as the tears flowed and the sense of loss began to wash over us all.

Later in the waiting room, I offered to be of further assistance to the family if I could, realizing that my work had been accomplished for the most part and that I, too, was physically and emotionally exhausted. Just as I was leaving, however, the nurse on duty stopped me and said, "Chaplain, there's a critical situation in the OB (obstetrics) unit. You'd better get up there right away."

As I entered the nursing station on the OB floor, I was struck by the frantic look of the staff and the desperate feel of the situation. Saying very little, I simply stood at the desk and listened. The stories came flooding out. An attending nurse indicated she thought the baby was dead as soon as it was born. Another disagreed, saying she had detected signs of life. Still another wondered how the mother should be told the news. The physician pored over the ECG graph and murmured, "It doesn't make a lick of sense," and then gave me that strange and menacing look I have often had directed my way in the past, as if to say, "How do you explain this, Reverend?" The baby, it seemed, had not survived, but had died shortly after birth. It was obvious that there was little I could do, other than simply to be there and allow people to bounce or project off me. I felt waves of hostility, concern, confusion, fright, cynicism, consolation, and yes, even hope, from close to a dozen different people whom I had never met before.

I was struck by the fact that, during the whole evening at the hospital, I had actually said very little. But I had been privileged to be present in the face of death itself—the death of an elderly woman who had presumably led a full life and the death of an infant who had never had a chance at life. I didn't need to comment or say much of anything: I simply needed to be present.

Questions regarding the meaning of death seem to come from all sides, often when we least expect it. Whether we serve as parish priests, ministers on call, hospice chaplains, lay visitors, healing ministers, healthcare ethics committee members, part-time pastors, or full-time chaplains on large hospital staffs, we are inevitably perplexed, sobered and grounded in humility as we encounter the physical death of another human being. Each death challenges and yet reaffirms our understanding of faith and Christian belief.

This and other responses from priests, chaplains, and lay ministers to the request of the End of Life Task Force for information reveal that ministry to those approaching death today has many novel dimensions. One of the most significant new roles that ministers are asked to serve is that of medical ethics consultant. Ethical decisions must be made within healthcare institutions that threaten to overwhelm patients, caregivers, and pastoral caregivers with their weight and complexity. Some of these decisions can seem fairly straightforward to those looking in from outside, as when the family above came to accept that their mother would not recover and that they could offer her a peaceful death free from further intrusions of medical technology. Yet even such apparently simple ethical decisions can be emotionally draining and may haunt those who make them for years afterward. More complex situations in which the ethical issue is not yet clear because the facts are elusive, such as the second above in which there was a question about whether more should have been done to keep a newborn alive, create even greater personal, emotional, and intellectual stress for patients, families, and ministers.

Clergy who are invited into the midst of such situations of choice and chance feel called to bring not only the sacraments of the Church and a sense of pastoral caring, but also an understanding of how Christian ethical insights can frame the choices to be made. It can be difficult for patients and their families to discern the concrete shape of an ethical understanding amid the complexities and uncertainties of actual events. At times, the nature of the illness may not be established, the course of a disease may be unforeseeable, and the success of treatment may be unpredictable. Moreover, obligations flowing from Christian ethical insights may seem to conflict in what they require or prohibit in these already perplexing situations. Those involved may experience deep moral uncertainty and anguish about choices they cannot avoid making. In such situations, ministers can help them to attempt to resolve the ethical issues at hand. They can lead them to accept themselves as finite and contingent beings, give them permission to acknowledge their limits, and remind them that theirs is the ethical responsibility of creatures, not of gods.[2]

At still other times, patients and families face decisions that are difficult, not because such choices are ethically agonizing and complex, but because those making them are leery about being candid with healthcare professionals. They may feel that professional staff within hospitals are caught up in institutional and role-related boundaries and are therefore inaccessible to them. As a consequence, patients may be reluctant to reveal their expectations, their convictions, and their ethical concerns to these professional caregivers. And healthcare professionals, too, may be reluctant to open themselves to the anguish of helping patients near the end of life grapple with hard ethical choices. Although their amazing skills and knowledge equip them to intervene into the processes of disease and dying, they may feel less adept at deciding when to stop aggressive treatment and simply keep company with patients as they die.

Ministers of the Church are often asked for ethical and pastoral help in all of these varied sorts of situations. They can respond by assisting patients and their families to reclaim their experience of dying and to bring it back within the ambit of the moral vision they share with the community of faith. Further, they can offer healthcare professionals an opportunity to recognize their special ministry to those approaching death and to help them to develop a sense of how to respond to patients with Christian ethical commitments. Although these roles are not wholly new to ministers, they take on new shapes and twists, new complications, sorrows, and joys, in the face of the contemporary healthcare environment.

Ministers find that they also need to be ready to deal with responses from dying patients that tear at the heart of their faith. Anger about the approach of death within an impersonal institutional setting can boil up from within the depths of patients or family caregivers. This can make communication difficult, if not impossible. The following unusual but telling story reveals the distance that can separate the dying from those around them. It also conveys some of the realities of ministering to the dying within the contemporary hospital.

> One of the most vivid yet painful experiences for me occurred when I sought to bring Communion to a dying man in an ICU who was strapped to a hospital gurney, apparently against his will, as he received (futile?) dialysis. Fighting the restraints, screaming and moaning desperately, attempting to pull away the sticking bandages and plastic tubes piercing his body, he cried out, "Leave me alone! Let me go!"
>
> I checked first at the nurse's station to see what was going on here, whether more could be done for the man and whether Communion was appropriate. I was told "He's unmanageable" and "It's up to you, Father." I proceeded to the bay, assured at least in my own mind that I would be welcomed as Christ's ambassador at the man's deathbed. "Take your [bleep] Communion kit, and get the [bleep] out of here!" he screamed. The man died within the hour of my visit.
>
> Even though the elements were never consecrated and distributed according to the prescribed rubrics, my attempt to share the broken body of Christ and to be a visible presence at the time of death was in keeping with the pastoral challenge to be faithful to the very end.

Although this priest was not able to provide the kind of succor and support he had planned and realized that it was too late to protest the patient's treatment, he had nevertheless been present to the dying man. A ministerial presence of this sort may evoke responses of anger, fear, dependence, or awe. It also may be the source of comfort and consolation in the face of current healthcare realities. In the end, another priest observes, "I have found the most significant contribution I can offer at the time of death is 'presence,' the fact that I am there; not what I say or what I do." Being present by honoring what is happening in the midst of death and dying is at the heart of both witnessing to and bearing God's presence.

Clergy serve those near death and those who care for them in many other ways as well. They are guides and advocates, shepherds, pastors, and spiritual directors. These distinctive roles are, of course, not unique to clergy. Other persons inside and outside Christian congregations can also assume them. Such individuals may bear a uniquely powerful presence and compelling witness precisely because they are simply fellow human beings and fellow Christians. Still, the responsibility of ordained clergy to uphold and support the ministry to those near the end of life, which is given to all by virtue of being Christian, is unique.

As guides and advocates, clergy are sources of information. In addition to providing written materials that may be useful to those who are seriously ill and dying, clergy are often the liaisons with other persons who can provide them with support and care. They may, for example, refer persons who face death to mental health professionals, support groups, social services, or legal counsel. In seeking such connections, clergy sometimes find that they need to serve as advocates for a patient or a family. This may be a matter of directly calling someone or setting up a consultation where questions about appropriate care can be clearly addressed. In bringing together these various persons, clergy bring a sense of caring to what might otherwise be, for those approaching death, an impersonal, institutional healthcare experience.

Where they serve congregations, clergy are shepherds of the community. One of their roles is to ensure that those who are dying and those who care for them remain connected to the larger community. This is a matter of facilitating adequate channels of communication, honoring privacy while still informing others in the community about those in need.

Finally, clergy are pastors and spiritual directors. They have a particular responsibility to pray with others and to serve as guides in the spiritual journey. Those who are dying and those who surround them may be struggling to make sense of what is happening and may seek to deepen their lives in prayer. Clergy can help in such circumstances by naming the present struggle and thereby casting some light on how God is present.

They may suggest ways in which persons near death might deepen a sense of God's power and grace.

In order to support clergy and those who minister at the end of life in all of these ancient and novel roles, educational opportunities and resources need to be recognized and expanded within the Church. Current preparation for ministry includes a variety of opportunities for exploring ministry to the dying in today's healthcare climate. Courses in medical ethics, for instance, are becoming increasingly available within seminaries, as are other programs that grapple with the novel healthcare issues that ministers of the church must confront today. After an apparent hiatus, seminars and classes in ministry to the dying are being offered once again in seminaries. Field education provides seminary students with an opportunity to address ethical and pastoral matters that arise in the care of those facing death. And Clinical Pastoral Education (CPE) prepares persons for ministry by offering them the opportunity to assume the role of chaplain in actual and, at times, ethically perplexing situations. Continuing education resources that are focused on ethical and theological issues arising near the end of life need to increase for those already in the field. Clergy retreats, diocesan clergy gatherings, and local clergy circles of various sorts should provide opportunities to explore new ethical and pastoral issues focused on end-of-life care.

All of these varied offerings are important to the preparation and continuing development of clergy who have the ability to enable and support ministries to the dying and their loved ones. A focus on ethics, theology, and end-of-life care may be considered a "special interest," but it is not. All human beings will die. And they will need a pastoral presence at that time. The Church has a distinctive responsibility to ensure that ministry is offered to those near death that offers ethical, theological, spiritual, and practical support in the face of the new healthcare environment.

LITURGICAL NEEDS AND ANGLICAN RESOURCES

Clergy have indicated to the task force that many people today don't know what to do at funerals. Should they sit or stand up for a hymn? Should they speak to others after the service? Should they bear a sad countenance or rejoice because the person who has died has gone on to the greater life? Such confusion about what to do during rites for the dead has been termed "the ritual incompetence of mourners."[3] As a society, we have become less familiar with ritual ways of meeting the needs of those on the path to death and of those who love them. Rituals and practices meant for those approaching death that were once associated with the *ars moriendi*, or "art of dying," literature, seem to be disappearing from contemporary secular consciousness. Traditional norms for mourning appear near collapse, leaving individuals to deal with grief as they will.

Yet all communities, by their very nature, develop structured, symbolic, and corporate ways of addressing life crises, including those of death and dying. Such ritual forms hold a significant place in human life, for they express important communal concerns and values. They enable members of the community to find meaning in the universe and in their own lives.[4] Moreover, they provide a social framework for the full expression of human experience and for sharing that experience with others.

When dying can no longer be contained through human efforts, patients and families need ways to address that disturbing reality. Because people today are more likely to die in hospitals than at home, a new, secular, ritual framework for those who are dying is developing within such institutions. Those who decide to withdraw futile or burdensome life-sustaining treatment, knowing that death will follow, seek social support at this difficult time. In response, some healthcare professionals who serve in hospitals have attempted to develop novel medical protocols that provide standard routines to be followed when life-sustaining treatment is withdrawn. These protocols offer a structured way of going through the procedure of removing technological equipment that resembles a ritual, quasi-religious act.

One such protocol, for instance, has been created for the time when respiratory support is withdrawn from a patient who is not expected to survive. It provides specific steps and movements that doctors, nurses, and families are to follow as the respirator is removed.[5] The healthcare professional who created it describes a specific situation in which he carries out a variety of steps until the climactic Step Eight is reached. At that point:

> I put a clean towel over the ET tube so it is concealed; once the cuff is deflated, the tube can be removed and kept covered with the towel, which also gets most of the secretions that come up with the tube. The family is behind me because I withdraw from the bed first with the towel and tube and the family can now come forward to a loved one whose face is now entirely de-equipmentized (NG and ET gone). A nurse at the opposite side of the head of the bed has a damp washcloth and oral suction catheter. [In this particular case,] the family and nurse had tissues for extra secretions and tears. (It amazes me how often physicians or nurses do not anticipate the need for tissues and so make getting them a production, as if tears are a surprising sign of lack of control.) The family wiped his face. Death followed fifteen minutes later. The mother held her son's hand and cried and assured him that grandma would welcome him on the other side.

This complexly patterned way of removing life-sustaining treatment serves, in effect, as a sort of last rite for the dying. It becomes a contemporary secular liturgy meant to give meaning and support to those involved.

In another instance, a procedure known as "cardiopulmonary resuscitation" has been developed in hospitals to attempt to revive those who suffer a cardiopulmonary arrest. This stylized pattern of resuscitation has been brought into the home in recent years by emergency medical services personnel and knowledgeable laypersons. It is highly unlikely to succeed in that setting, however, for those who are near death. Even so, attempts at resuscitation have been undertaken for the dying in homes in order to give those close to them the comforting feeling that the person involved has been attended to and has died properly. These resuscitation procedures can also serve a function akin to that of a religious ritual.

Two doctors who tried to resuscitate a close relative at a family picnic describe their efforts.

> I kept listening for a siren, anything. We pumped and breathed away, the two doctors, providing what we optimistically call basic life-support but which, it was becoming apparent, was just a grisly sort of last rites. I remember thinking that all I was really doing was kissing Bethann good-bye . . .
>
> After Bethann died, Nancy and I both had flashbacks. We tortured ourselves with questions . . . Didn't we make her death a gruesome medicalized one instead of the mythically peaceful death that it could have been without our useless and brutal interventions? . . .
>
> But a funny thing happened. Everybody else told us how glad they were that we were there, and how comforting it was to know that Bethann had received CPR [cardiopulmonary resuscitation]. They had the feeling, in spite of the fact that she had died, that somehow she had died properly. We may have failed technically, but our ritual had succeeded . . .[6]

Certain structured medical procedures, this description reveals, are becoming our secular culture's desperate symbolic dance around the bed of those nearing death. They offer a ritual sanctification of the process of dying to those involved.

Anglicans need not fall back on such secular rituals in order to find meaning and support at the end of life. Yet they must address the fact that there is a need for such rituals in the novel circumstances in which death occurs today. The Church currently provides rites for the time surrounding death at two points: when the death of a person is imminent ("Ministration at the Time of Death," BCP, 462–467) and after death ("Burial I" and "Burial II," BCP, 468–507). In addition, the Prayer Book offers Prayers and Thanksgivings (BCP, 809–841) that can be adapted to give comfort and support in some of the circumstances in which individuals face death today. All of these prayers and rites are meant to focus attention on the concrete realities of dying at the point when death is imminent and uncontrollable and also on the actual death. They bring Christian affirmation and comfort to those who are making the transition from life to death and offer family, friends, and the community an opportunity to support them and express their beliefs, thoughts, and emotions in an accepting setting.

Unfortunately, the service of "Ministration to the Sick" (BCP, 453), with its prayers for healing, is not always recognized as appropriate for those who are near death and is therefore used less often than it could be. One clerical respondent to the task force whose ministry is especially devoted to those who are dying commented that:

> Our tradition has seemingly abdicated its responsibility to stand by the dying person's bedside in her official and visible form. The "Ministration at the Time of Death" is separated from the other rite ["Ministration to the Sick"]; no actions of anointing, laying on of hands, or offering of the Eucharist are suggested. The prayers are archaic, and a litany includes five different responses, which would require those present to be tied to a book or handout—not the kind of thing one is apt to do when someone is dying.

Other clergy find that Prayer Book resources for those approaching death must be pulled together from a variety of places, leaving them and those attending them with no one service that considers their need for healing and wholeness. Another minister discusses these difficulties:

> Much of my clerical time with those who know that they are near life's end is spent trying to figure out what fits the context of their situation most helpfully. Is an anointing, or "last rites" of some type, in order? "Ministration at the Time of Death"? Or would that be counterproductive, scaring people instead of reassuring and affirming them? Are prayers needed—and if so, which ones? Should they be prayers from the Prayer Book, spontaneous prayers, extemporaneous prayers, silent prayers; or other more timely readings? Should we hold hands, touch the dying, or simply stand in a circle around the bedside offering verbal ministrations? Should we, perhaps more appropriately, be prepared to get out of the way? What if it's a sudden death and the body has collapsed in a grotesque position on the floor, and we're still waiting for the coroner? Should we handle or move anything, cover the body out of respect (To whom? So who won't have to see it?), or should we lend assistance to the medics in lifting, literally, dead weight?

As this comment indicates, current rituals do not address some of the changed circumstances that people face today as they approach the end of life. The service of "Ministration to the Sick" includes no prayers for the person who learns unexpectedly that he or she is terminally ill and will die within the next few months. It provides no prayers for someone who must make difficult choices from among a variety of miserable treatment options. No prayers are given for an individual who learns that a series of treatments has been only partially successful and has merely delayed the onset of dying. None can be found for a patient who comes to accept that death is very near and that life-sustaining treatment should be withdrawn. And there are no prayers for a person enrolled in hospice care. In short, the Church has no specific prayers for those who learn that they are terminally ill, nor does it have resources that explicitly take account of those diagnosed with a chronic illness that will ultimately lead to death.

Thus, there are significant gaps among existing liturgical resources of the Church for those who are approaching death. There is also a lack of clarity about when and how current liturgies can and should be used. Consequently, some persons who learn that they will die at a certain point in the future must live out their remaining time in relative isolation with little liturgical support from the Church. This troubles clergy and laypersons as they strive to witness to Christ's love for those who cope with the experience of dying today, especially those within institutionalized healthcare settings.

If we are to address these gaps and gain a meaningful liturgical direction for the future, we need to provide not only currently available rituals for those near the end of life but also expanded and new rites that capture the realities of dying in today's healthcare environment. These need to reflect the theology of healing that the Church expresses in the 1979 edition of *The Book of Common Prayer*, rather than the somewhat punitive view of sickness expressed in earlier editions of the Prayer Book. Thus, these rituals should emphasize the love and healing power of God, recognizing that healing for those who are dying has a broader purpose than bodily recovery—that of wholeness in God. Moreover, these resources would take into account the current realities of dying as closely as do the secular rituals described above. Rev. Dr. Leonel Mitchell recognizes about our liturgies in general that:

> We cannot expect simply to revive the rituals of the early Church, for we do not live in the patristic era any more than we do in the Middle Ages or the nineteenth century. Medieval Christendom adopted, adapted, and thereby profoundly changed the rituals of the early Church, which it preserved. We must do the same.[7]

Traditional materials have not lost their resonance. Yet new liturgies need to reflect the idiom and usage of the time and culture for which they are intended.

This understanding underlies the work of the current Standing Commission on Liturgy and Music. Through its Expansive Language Committee, the standing commission has devoted time and effort to revising and expanding services of the Episcopal Church that are related to those approaching death. It has revised "Ministry to the Sick and Dying" to encompass prayers for those who are dying, and it has created a new rite, "Burial of a Child," to fill one gap in current liturgical offerings of the

Church. These services retain familiar petitions for the sick and also introduce new prayers from a variety of Anglican and ecumenical sources. They are not intended to supersede but to supplement current services that are available. We believe that the efforts of the standing commission are to be applauded and that they ought to be considered seriously and prayerfully.

In addition, the Committee on Medical Ethics of the Diocese of Washington has created a service known as "A Form of Prayer for a Time When Life-Sustaining Treatment Is Withdrawn."[8] It offers consolation and support for all of those—patients, family, friends, and healthcare professionals—involved in the difficult act of removing medical technology that no longer offers hope of benefit. This brief service was developed with the assistance of the late Rev. Dr. Charles Price and uses language that is simple, familiar, and expressive to address a critical pastoral need. The service, which has been adopted in draft form with modifications by the Standing Commission on Liturgy and Music, appears in the appendix of this book in its original form.

The privilege of offering these prayers and rites that surround the end of life should be granted to the laity as fully as possible. As we observed in the previous chapter, all baptized persons can assume a role on behalf of the Church in discharging many of the congregation's pastoral responsibilities. Placing a layperson at the bedside of any Church member who is near death can offer a significant form of spiritual support to that person. Laypersons, for instance, can lead such services as "A Form of Prayer for a Time When Life-Sustaining Treatment Is Withdrawn." Given the need to facilitate effective, timely, and more frequent use of the service of "Laying on of Hands and Anointing" (BCP, 455), greater use might be made of the provision for laity to anoint the dying with oil blessed by a bishop or priest (BCP, 456).

Not only the Church but our healthcare system as a whole is called to develop greater resources in order to respond to those who are approaching death. Questions are being raised about whether this system is leaving behind a substantial number of people who either receive inadequate care from within it or else fall outside its auspices altogether. In particular, there is concern about what policies we should adopt to ensure that those approaching death gain access to our healthcare system and receive desperately needed palliative care. We now turn to these issues.

---

1. A book of materials entitled *Deacons in Hospital Chaplaincy* prepared by Rev. Robert Bruckart and Ven. Linda J. Brondstedt for the Institute for Christian Studies, The School of Diaconal Training, The Diocese of Central Florida, contains sections not only on spiritual and religious concerns, but also on the following: crisis intervention (describing the emergency department and critical care units); end-of-life issues (including information about advance directives and planning one's funeral); hospice; ethical issues (including a bioethics training manual that covers such matters as ethics committees, landmark legal cases, patient's

bill of rights, policies concerning resuscitation and brain death, patient abuse, organizational ethics); neonatal issues; pediatric issues; organ and tissue donation. For further information, contact Rev. Robert Bruckart, Director of Pastoral Care, Homes Regional Medical Center, 1350 S. Hickory St., Melbourne, FL 32901. His phone number is (407) 434-7000.

2. Sondra Ely Wheeler, *Stewards of Life: Bioethics and Pastoral Care* (Nashville: Abingdon Press, 1996), 19–35.

3. Tony Walter, *The Revival of Death,* (New York and London: Routledge, 1994), 17.

4. Leonel L. Mitchell, *The Meaning of Ritual* (Harrisburg, Pa: Morehouse Publishing, 1977), 14.

5. Steve Miles, "Protocol for Rapid Withdrawal of Ventilator Support in Anticipation of Death," *Ethical Currents,* No. 45 (Spring, 1996), 1, 6–7.

6. John D. Lantos, "Bethann's Death," *Hastings Center Report* 25:2 (1995), 22–23.

7. Mitchell, *The Meaning of Ritual,* 128.

8. See Appendix 4.

CHAPTER 8

BROADENING THE CONVERSATION

From the beginning, Christians have been moved by a vision of what faithful living and faithful dying mean and have acted to meet the needs of those approaching death. They have established practices and institutional structures that offer comfort and support to the dying. The early Church, following the lead of Jesus, appointed ministers to visit, pray with, and anoint the sick and the dying. When Christianity later became the established faith of the Roman Empire, the Church created institutions to address the physical, spiritual, and emotional needs of those near death and supported the growth of the healing professions.[1] Basil the Great saw in the fourth century that while charity called Christians to serve individuals who were ill and their families, the prevailing social order made this difficult to accomplish. Basil therefore established monastic houses that cared for lepers. These communities, which were the beginnings of the hospital, were places of welcome for those who were sick and had no one to care for them. Thus, Christians have always been committed to offering compassionate care for those who are sick and approaching death as a significant way of imitating Christ and of expressing their concern for the dignity of vulnerable persons and for the common good.

Similarly, the Church is called today to bring its voice to bear in the attempt to ensure that all people receive decent and appropriate primary health care in their living and their dying. We currently face the fearful possibility that those near death will have their dying prolonged by modern medical technology and yet will not receive sufficient pain relief, comfort, and support during that time. The Anglican moral vision, with its emphasis on the Church as a corporate body of which each of us is an integral and cherished member, bids us to embody and express the values that are distinctive of our way of life. As a matter of love and justice, the Church is called upon to address the challenge that the lack of adequate palliative care in the United States and around the world presents to those endeavoring to live and die faithfully and to those caring for them.

Therefore, in this chapter the task force explores the important ethical and policy question of how to provide access to palliative care and pain relief within our healthcare system for those who are approaching death. Whereas earlier in chapters 4 and 5 we discussed several significant ethical questions that arise for individuals and the community surrounding them near the end of life, here we focus on how the wider society can meet the ethical imperative to provide adequate supportive care for the dying. We do so by considering ways in which current policy creates barriers to comfort care for those who are dying and how we can overcome these so that those approaching death can gain such care. Our goal is not to resolve completely the policy problems related to the end of life—for they are extremely complex—but to move toward their resolution by addressing them in Christian and, specifically, Anglican terms. Persons whose lives are coming to an end need to be assured that the Church cares about them and is working to help them live out their remaining days in faith, comfort, dignity, and peace.

THE CONTEXT: A CRISIS IN U.S. HEALTHCARE POLICY

Obstacles to providing adequate palliative care for those near the end of life have not arisen in a vacuum but have been created by policy choices that have drawn the shape of the current healthcare system in the United States. In order to understand why there is only limited palliative care available to the dying, we need first to grasp why there is a crisis in the way that health care is provided in this country today.

By *policy*, we mean what governments and organizations say and do about matters they wish to affect.[2] These bodies authorize certain actions by individuals and organizations and limit or constrain other actions of theirs through the policies they adopt. Thus, policy significantly affects the healthcare choices that can be made by individual patients and healthcare professionals; it also establishes the boundaries within which healthcare organizations, employers, and insurers must work. Policies play a pivotal role in determining whether the distribution of resources within and without our healthcare system is just and whether such services as palliative care are available and adequate.

Ours is a healthcare system—if indeed it can be called a system—that most observers agree is in crisis. It is vast, terribly complex, and almost ubiquitous in its effects. Moreover, it permeates every sector of our economy, employing millions of people and accounting for annual expenditures of almost one trillion dollars, or approximately 15 percent of our gross domestic product. This unwieldy system touches almost every individual in the country at some point through encounters with healthcare professionals, healthcare organizations, and private or state-sponsored insurance programs.

However, our healthcare system touches these individuals in very inconsistent ways.[3] This is because it is also extremely fragmented. That is, it provides care in a variety of different settings that have no systemic connection with one another. Healthcare analysts describe this by saying that the healthcare system fails to provide a "continuum of care" for the patients, clients, and residents who are its ultimate "customers." The system is also highly bureaucratized, using ever-larger numbers of officials to administer huge and unwieldy healthcare structures that often fail to respond appropriately to the needs of patients. And, finally, this system, which is more market-oriented than any other major health system in the industrialized world, is so irrationally regulated that many healthcare professionals and patients are not aware of the financial consequences of their decisions. They thus tend to be unresponsive to efforts to curb the steadily rising costs of health care, for they cannot grasp the economic impact of their individual choices on the system as a whole.

The current crisis in our healthcare system is the direct result of our inability to slow spiraling healthcare costs. This has been of mounting concern because the size of the share of national resources devoted to healthcare threatens to diminish funds available for other important areas of our civil life, such as education, housing, and defense. Policy analysts have identified a number of causes for these increasing healthcare costs. One is the massive amount of high-technology research produced by government, university, and industry laboratories. This results in costly new applications that are marketed to a public eager for the latest, often more expensive medical breakthroughs.[4] Spiraling costs also result from the bureaucratization and fragmentation of our healthcare system noted above. Bureaucratization drives up administrative costs, and fragmentation often forces patients to seek treatment in more expensive settings than are necessary for their condition. Fraud, abuse, and waste are also said to account for 10–15 percent of unnecessary healthcare costs each year.

These rising costs have a direct impact on the pressing policy issue of concern here: access to palliative care at the end of life. Because spending on care at the end of life is large and because much of it is financed by government programs, the cost of end-of-life care has attracted considerable attention.

WHY PALLIATIVE CARE IS OF CONCERN TO PUBLIC POLICY MAKERS

As we observed in chapter 1, faithful living calls us to cherish life and to strive to live fully with a good quality of life. We want this not only for our own sake but also for that of our families, friends, and associates. However, if we are severely injured, extremely sick, or in a debilitating chronic condition leading to death, we may well be forced to make a hard choice between extending our dying through painful interventions or living a shorter time in relative comfort.

Such difficult decisions have perhaps always been part of the human condition. Most agree, however, that they have reached particular urgency and poignancy today because advances in medicine have given us greater control over illness and the timing of death. This control, and the extension of the dying process to which it can lead, give rise to the need for more adequate palliative care so that those who decide against prolonging their dying can be assured that their pain and suffering will be alleviated. When treatment is no longer beneficial, patients should not have to fear that they will be abandoned to a painful death. Current medical and nursing capabilities should be sufficient to provide them with appropriate palliative care to ease them through the process of faithful dying.

Let us return to a discussion of palliative care here, considering it in terms of public policy. Palliative care, according to the National Hospice Organization, is "treatment that enhances comfort and improves the quality of the patient's life."[5] This form of care can not only make persons more comfortable as they die but can also provide a way of dying that is less expensive than that afforded by high-technology medicine. Since family members can often be trained to provide the services needed near life's end, palliative care reduces the need for funds to pay professional caregivers. Moreover, these services can usually be given in less costly settings than, say, the intensive care unit of a hospital. It has been estimated that if end-of-life palliative care were delivered across the country through a hospice program, this would not only provide greater patient comfort but would also save about 3.3 percent of all healthcare expenditures—a significant amount of money.[6] Thus, it seems obvious to many observers that palliative care should be readily provided and easily accessible in our healthcare system as a matter of policy, so as to give comfort and support in an economical way to those who are dying. This, however, is not the case.

PROBLEMS OF ACCESS TO HEALTH CARE IN GENERAL AND PALLIATIVE CARE IN PARTICULAR

There is a significant problem of access to health care in general within the United States. This, in turn, has had a negative impact on access to palliative care. The term *access* refers to whether people can get treatment when they need it. *Access* also has to do with how readily they can become "entitled," either through right or contract, to receive healthcare services. Factors such as whether individuals have health insurance and have available affordable care are often discussed in terms of access. In order to understand what is at issue when it is said that there is a problem of access to palliative care, a very brief overview of our healthcare system and who has access to it today, will be helpful.

It is estimated that, at any one time, more than 40 million U.S. citizens do not have health insurance and that about 20 million more are under-insured. Since World War II, health insurance has been increasingly tied to employment. This creates special difficulties for some who, according to studies, can have difficulty finding employment, such as the working poor, members of minority groups, and single mothers. When such persons do obtain employment, they tend to work for small firms that often cannot afford to offer healthcare insurance to employees. Because of this, individuals in these groups are overrepresented among the millions lacking healthcare insurance.

At the basis of this problem of access to health care is a profound ambivalence about the role of government in addressing problems of health care. Instead of declaring health care a right and ensuring that all persons have equal access to such care, the United States has chosen to treat it in large part as a commodity or commercial product. And it is widely agreed that commodities are better provided by the market than by the government. This approach to health care implies that it ought to be allocated like any other commodity—on the basis of our ability to pay for it. However, almost no one can now afford to pay for his or her own health care.

In response, rather than declaring health care a right and financing it directly with taxes, the United States has chosen to finance health care through a complex combination of private and public insurance programs. Our *de facto* policy seems to be this: the government will use the private insurance market whenever possible to distribute health care and will then address any remaining gaps through public or government-sponsored programs. The key to access, therefore, *seems* to be to provide private or public health insurance coverage for those millions who are now excluded from it. The problem with this conclusion, however, is that our current system of insurance is one of the principal reasons that healthcare costs are spiraling out of control! To get a sense of why this is the case, we will consider briefly how health insurance has come to function for individuals who are deciding about what medical options to choose.

Traditional health insurance did not provide those making a decision about medical treatment (primarily patients and physicians) with an opportunity to compare the cost of the treatment to its value. Yet this is an opportunity that consumers need to have in an open market. If we think the price of an item is too high for the value we expect to realize from buying it, we can either walk away or try to negotiate a lower price. Under our former "fee-for-service" payment system, neither patients nor their physicians had an incentive to walk away or to negotiate, for they were assured that the cost of care would be covered by patients' insurance.

Further, patients presumably needed the health care they were seeking and were consequently unable to walk away. Yet often they did not have the information they needed to understand what they were buying or how costly it was. For their part, physicians had no reason even to ask about the price of health care. Indeed, they were concerned that knowing the price of their treatment recommendations might lead them to compromise their professional judgment.

Under the traditional fee-for-service system of healthcare financing, physicians had an incentive to give patients as much treatment as they needed—and more. Insurance companies merely passed the costs through to employers or government agencies in the form of increased premiums. But both employers and legislators who represented the taxpayers funding government programs found they were having an increasingly difficult time paying for health insurance. Costs reached the point where almost everyone was crying, "Enough!" This was when managed care was introduced into our healthcare system.

Managed care reverses the incentive structures under which health care had been financed earlier. Managed care organizations pay providers—physician groups or integrated systems that deliver health care—for the number of "covered lives" or "members" they serve, rather than for each treatment. They give each provider a certain dollar amount per member per month and that provider is expected to pay all costs incurred for treating patients from the total amount received. The funds that remain are kept by the provider.

Thus, *in principle,* our societal decision to change to managed care was a good one, for it was designed to provide needed care at a reasonable cost. Employers embraced it, at least initially, because when they switched their employee health benefits from fee-for-service to managed care programs their insurance costs either leveled off or went down. Physicians also liked it initially. Managed care organizations gave them an incentive to keep their patients well, which is what they were trained to do. Further, physicians were in control of their patients' care, and if they could attract healthy patients or keep their patients healthy, they might receive greater financial benefits than they did under the old fee-for-service system. And many patients liked managed care. It removed the incentive to "overtreat"—or to provide too much treatment to the point that it might harm patients. Under managed care, patients' out-of-pocket expenses also went down and their payments were easier for them to understand. Indeed, except for their copayments, they rarely saw a bill.

In practice, however, the results of managed care have been somewhat disappointing. One reason is that as soon as managed care organizations achieve a dominant presence in a particular market, they begin to lower their payments to physicians and other providers and to raise their fees to employers and government funding agencies. In this way, managed care organizations use the power they gain from having a considerable share of the healthcare market to increase profits. In addition, they set up cumbersome administrative hurdles that physicians and patients must negotiate to gain approval to purchase treatments. These hurdles greatly increase the administrative burdens of physicians, driving up their costs at the very time they are receiving less money for each patient. Many physicians also believe that they are losing control of medical decision making under managed care because they must spend a good deal of time negotiating with less skilled professionals about what care is appropriate and can be authorized. At the same time, we have seen a consumer outcry against managed care, and heard anecdotal stories of the denial of care with horrible— but avoidable—outcomes.[7]

Thus, we now have enough experience to conclude—tentatively, at least—that managed care is not so much keeping healthcare costs down as distributing the profits of the earlier system in a different way. In other words, by offering lower costs to employers and to government agencies who contract with them for healthcare coverage, managed care organizations are initially able to achieve a genuine *one-time* saving of healthcare dollars. However, once managed care reaches a higher level of market dominance, physicians and healthcare institutions find their payments decreasing and employers and funding agencies find their costs increasing. Managed care organizations move the savings they achieve to their own bottom line whenever they can in order to achieve greater profits. And, if we believe health care is merely a commodity, there may be nothing wrong with this— it's just good business. But, if we instead view health care as a right, as did the Seventieth General Convention of the Episcopal Church in 1991 when it asserted "the right of all individuals to medically necessary healthcare,"[8] we will become concerned about the commodification of health care.

How do these problems with our healthcare system affect the ability of patients to gain access to palliative care and of healthcare professionals to offer it? Those who are near death may be adversely affected by the financial arrangements that exist under managed care plans. Because our population is growing and aging and because end-of-life care expenses have increased along with the general costs of medical treatment, care for those near the end of life is having a noticeable impact on healthcare costs. About 20–30 percent of healthcare costs are expended on end-of-life treatment. Yet efforts to decrease these costs by lowering funds available to those approaching death raises a concern that the dying will carry a disproportionately heavy burden of the effort to cut the costs of health care. Some fear that current public and private managed care policies may lead to the discharge of those near death from healthcare institutions before this is medically appropriate and before they have time to arrange for palliative and other forms of care. Financial arrangements under managed care may therefore have a negative impact on those who are dying. Moreover, those who are without healthcare insurance often have no access to palliative care and other forms of health care near the end of life. This is a matter of great concern to those who believe that we owe those who are approaching death the assurance that they will not be abandoned but will receive care and comfort at the end of life's journey.

THINKING ABOUT OUR POLICIES CONCERNING END-OF-LIFE CARE IN CHRISTIAN TERMS

A major thrust of the Anglican moral vision of death and dying is that all patients and families should have access to palliative care near the end of life. The Sixty-Ninth General Convention of the Episcopal Church recognized this moral mandate in 1989 when it called for "a strategy to advocate for all persons suffering from illness by creating appropriate levels of cost-effective healthcare, for example, hospices and alternative healthcare facilities."[9] This statement recognizes not only that it is morally essential to provide palliative care to those who are sick and suffering out of compassion but also that such care can be cost-effective in a society that is attempting to limit healthcare costs.

Up to the present, however, massive economic and political forces have been arrayed against resolving the problems associated with palliative care out of an interest in safeguarding the bottom line and in making political accommodations. Many major decision makers, such as insurance companies and managed care systems, have vested interests in keeping the current arrangements in place. Most important, the American public seems to have little interest in changing the system, especially if that would result in increased taxes. Still, we have an obligation, as Christians who stand in a family relationship as creatures of God, to care for those who are sick and in need. The Committee on Medical Ethics of the Diocese of Washington points out that:

> Caring for the vulnerable and dying is one of the significant ways in which we can respond to the call to emulate Christ. The community has a responsibility to assist those who cannot take care of their own health because of poverty, age, or disability. We are not isolated individuals who must always stand alone on our own two feet, regardless of circumstances. Instead, we are dependent on one another and bound out of love of Christ to help one another to meet our basic needs.[10]

Thus, we are called to recommend that all persons within our country, especially those who are dying, have access to the healthcare system, including appropriate forms of palliative care. Those who are unable to afford such care should be protected against a miserable death by means of governmental and institutional arrangements. Those who are well and well-off have an obligation to rise above self-interest and, recognizing the worth of each person in the sight of God, to subsidize palliative care for the poor and uninsured who are dying. Moreover, we have an obligation to make palliative care available not only to those known to be terminally ill but also to those with a chronic condition that will lead to death.

With these obligations in mind, how are we to analyze and evaluate current healthcare policy in Christian terms? We can proceed by using what ethicists call a "mixed approach."[11] This begins by adopting methodologies that are basically *consequentialist* in their structure. That is, they consider results—how well health policy actually brings about certain valued states of affairs or how well it probably will bring them about. These methodologies assume that there is some good or goods that ought to be maximized or promoted. In the case of healthcare policy for those approaching death, that good would be that all persons living within the United States have access to appropriate and affordable end-of-life care.

However, consequentialist methods are notoriously difficult to delimit and constrain. For example, we might promote access to appropriate and affordable end-of-life care without considering the effects of our actions on, say, the defense budget or education. Thus, boundaries need to be drawn around the use of consequentialist methodologies by bringing "deontic" considerations to bear on the conclusions reached by such methodologies. *Deontic considerations* encompass certain ethical, social, and spiritual values that are considered intrinsically good, or good in themselves. Human dignity is an example of one deontic value that is of great significance both to secular society and to Christians. In using the "mixed approach," we consider whether there are certain deontic values that keep us from acting on the conclusions of our initial consequentialist analysis. Thus, for example, we realize that we are constrained from deliberately killing those diagnosed with a terminal illness, no matter how much good might result for others from the action, because this would be a gross violation of the basic deontic value, human dignity.

This said, Christians might differentiate their evaluations of health policy from those of others with regard to:

- the *particular results or states of affairs* they wish to see promoted by health policy;
- how those results are *ranked* relative to others when they compete or conflict; and
- *a particular set of deontic values that serve as constraints* on agents in the pursuit of these results or states of affairs.

We say Christians "might" differentiate their evaluations in this way because they will undoubtedly share many assessments with non-

Christians. Also, Christians must recognize that current health policy constrains what they—or anyone, for that matter—can do to bring about the results that they value. That is, Christians must account realistically for the larger economic and political forces that already exist or that would be likely to develop if they were to begin some concerted effort to affect health policy.

This last observation points to the importance of what Catholic moral theologian, Richard A. McCormick, S.J., discusses as the "feasibility criterion."[12] He means by this that Christians who are seeking to affect public policy must recognize that what is morally ideal in Christian terms is not always economically, politically, or—given our pluralism and secular state—culturally and legally possible. Thus, Christians must also *decide where they can and cannot compromise* when they interact with lobbyists, legislators, and powerful business interests.[13]

In an effort to take seriously the task of articulating a vision for U.S. health care that is rooted in Christian values, the End of Life Task Force believes that the Episcopal Church, as a significant Christian body, ought to consider proceeding as follows. First, Church leaders should decide what priority to give healthcare policy in general. By this we mean they should decide where healthcare policy ranks in terms of the Church's internal concerns and also where healthcare policy ought to be ranked by public policy makers. The assertion by the Seventieth General Convention of "the right of all individuals to medically necessary healthcare" indicates that the Episcopal Church gives a considerable degree of importance to healthcare policy. As a practical matter, however, Church leaders must also decide whether they can muster the resources to make a difference in this area of public policy. They will need to recognize that policy makers have other significant issues to attend to in addition to healthcare policy, and they will therefore need to bring the Church's view of its importance to the attention of these public servants with a degree of intensity that is reasonable.

Second, if the Church decides that healthcare policy has sufficient priority to warrant some allocation of its resources, Episcopalians should next try to reach as much consensus as possible among themselves on (1) the results that they believe the Church should seek, based on their understanding of the Christian tradition, and (2) the deontic constraints on these results that emerge from Christian teaching and that are "non-negotiable." For both of these efforts, the task force recommends that the Church try to make more explicit a relatively small set of principles, values, or criteria that can be used to evaluate *any* healthcare policy proposal, no matter its source. These criteria ought to be defensible in Christians terms and, ideally, in secular (i.e., humanistic) terms as well, if they are to have a chance of gaining support outside the Christian community. (Support from other religious groups should also be solicited, especially other Christian groups, and Jewish, Muslim, and other bodies as well.)

Some of the principles and values that are likely to emerge from this discussion have been articulated over the history of the Christian, particularly the Anglican, tradition, and in past statements issued by the General Convention of the Episcopal Church. Thus, the Christian tradition teaches that its adherents ought to follow the example of Jesus and provide care to those who are sick and in need. The tradition further indicates that basic health care ought to be available to all, because all are created in the image of God, and because individual health is an important condition for realizing the common good. Although maintenance of physical life is a very important good, as we have stated earlier, it is not an absolute good that outweighs all other goods. Efforts to restore health ought to be guided by the human purposes of the whole person as a physical, emotional, and spiritual unity.

The Episcopal Church, in light of this tradition, has affirmed a number of specific principles for the U.S. healthcare system that are relevant to this discussion. The Seventy-First General Convention, for instance, adopted four principles regarding health care:

1. That universal access to quality, cost-effective healthcare services be considered necessary for everyone in the population;
2. That "quality healthcare" be defined so as to include programs in preventive medicine, where wellness is the first priority;
3. That "quality healthcare" include interdisciplinary and interprofessional components to insure the care of the whole person—physiological, spiritual, psychological, social;
4. That "quality healthcare" include the balanced distribution of resources so that no region of the country is underserved.[14]

A number of recent Christian authors have also considered the principles and values that should guide our healthcare policies. For example, Charles J. Doughtery, working from the Roman Catholic tradition, argues for the following guiding principles: respecting the dignity of human persons, offering care and compassion, protecting the least well off, serving the common good, containing healthcare costs (stewardship), choosing responsibly, and promoting excellence or quality of care.[15] In our opinion, these teachings of the Christian tradition, Episcopal Church statements, and proposed guiding principles should be carefully considered and then synthesized to provide the core of the Church's response to the current crisis in healthcare policy.

Third, when consensus begins to emerge on key guiding principles and values, the Church should engage expert consultants to map their implications for crafting healthcare policy. First, these consultants should try to describe an ideal healthcare system that is consistent with the Church's principles and values. Second, they should suggest strategies to "nudge" the current system in the direction of this ideal, for surely it will be easier to adjust the current system than it will be to remake it *de novo*. Here, the Church, realizing that all the goods articulated may not be feasible and that compromise will need to be considered, would decide whether to support strategies to move the United States toward some of the following options:

- Adopting a policy of universal access to affordable health care, without regard to employment status, and, in the meanwhile, taking additional "stop gap" measures;
- Advocating a "tiered" healthcare system in which everyone is guaranteed a level of decent basic care, while some are permitted to receive more;
- Finding some ways of working with the private health insurance industry to achieve broader healthcare insurance coverage in recognition of the industry's market strength and historically important role in allocating and financing health care;
- Shifting society's resources from ineffective end-of-life "rescue care" to reasonable and cost-effective therapeutic, palliative, and preventive care.

We believe that with regard to end-of-life care, the Church should urge healthcare professionals, organizations, and policy makers to:

1. Support more adequate and comprehensive end-of-life care for *all* persons with a condition that will cause death in the foreseeable future, not restricting such care to the last six months of life.

2. Promote timely referrals to hospice for patients approaching the end of life who can benefit from this form of care.

3. Reform drug prescription laws, regulations, and state medical board policies and practices that impede the effective use of narcotics to relieve pain and suffering for those near the end of life.

4. Mandate, through appropriate accrediting bodies, adequate education in palliative care within medical schools, residency training programs, and nursing schools.

Finally, the Church should consider approaches that engage both the market and public policy more directly. We recommend that it foster the formation of an association of groups and individuals involved in healthcare policy. This association would include Episcopal healthcare organizations, the National Episcopal Health Ministries, the Assembly of Episcopal Healthcare Chaplains, Episcopalians developing or teaching healthcare policy, and other informed and interested groups and individuals within the Episcopal Church involved in healthcare policy. This organization would assist the Church in its efforts to:

1. Understand and keep abreast of the rapidly changing healthcare market and developments in biomedical research that affect health-related public policy, particularly with regard to end-of-life care.

2. Articulate and communicate Episcopal Church positions with

regard to healthcare policy, particularly with regard to end-of-life care, to public policy makers and to the public.

3. Advocate for a healthcare system that would guarantee decent and appropriate primary care and end-of-life care for all.

4. Develop resources and teaching materials related to access to health care for the use of dioceses, congregations, and individuals that might strengthen their position in the public policy arena and their communication with each other, particularly with regard to end-of-life care.

An organization such as this would represent the Church's collective efforts to re-enter the healthcare fray in terms of the market, national and state politics, and, most important, its own vision for a more just, compassionate, and rational healthcare system.

---

1. See Darrel W. Amundsen, *Medicine, Society, and Faith in the Ancient and Medieval Worlds* (Baltimore: Johns Hopkins University Press, 1995).

2. Adapted from Randall B. Ripley and Grace A. Franklin, *Congress, the Bureaucracy, and Public Policy,* 5th ed. (Pacific Grove, Calif.: Books/Cole Publishing Company, 1991), 1. This book provides a very good description of public policy formation and the types of policy developed on the federal level. It informs much of what is said here.

3. See the classic study by Paul Starr, *The Social Transformation of American Medicine: The Rise of a Sovereign Profession and the Making of a Vast Industry* (New York: Basic Books, 1982).

4. This observation needs some qualification. Medical technology has done great good and, in many cases, contributes to lowering healthcare costs. What is problematic, however, is the use of this technology when it provides little or no therapeutic benefit at the end of life. Another concern is that there is unequal access to it, even when it can be therapeutically beneficial.

5. Porter Storey and Carol F. Knight, *UNIPAC Six: Ethical and Legal Decision Making When Caring for the Terminally Ill* (Gainesville, Fla.: American Academy of Hospice and Palliative Medicine, 1996), 9.

6. Ezekiel J. Emanuel and Linda L. Emanuel, "The Economics of Dying: The Illusion of Cost Savings at the End of Life," *New England Journal of Medicine,* vol. 330, No. 8, 1994, 540–544.

7. For a detailed discussion of the impact of managed care on patients, see Committee on Medical Ethics, Diocese of Washington, *Toward a Good Christian Death: Crucial Treatment Choices,* (Harrisburg, Pa.: Morehouse, 1999), Appendix B, "The Changing Healthcare System and Managed Care," 118–125.

8. Reprinted in *Toward a Good Christian Death,* 130.

9. Idem.

10. Ibid., 108.

11. See Rosemarie Tong, *Ethics in Policy Analysis* (Englewood Cliffs, N.J.: Prentice-Hall, 1986).

12. See Richard A. McCormick, S.J., "Theology in the Public Forum," in Richard A. McCormick, S.J., *The Critical Calling: Reflections on Moral Dilemmas Since Vatican II* (Washington, D.C.: Georgetown University Press, 1989), 191–208.

13. Their only other option is to enter the market and the political arena in a *major* way, and there are many barriers to this strategy at this point in time, though Episcopalians might consider "strategic partnerships" with other Christians still in the healthcare market as a way of affecting policy. They might also take steps to strengthen and expand those Episcopalian healthcare entities that remain in the market.

14. Reprinted in *Toward a Good Christian Death,* 131.

15. Charles J. Dougherty, *Back to Reform: Values, Markets, and the Healthcare System* (New York: Oxford University Press, 1996).

FINAL REFLECTIONS

Throughout this book, the End of Life Task Force has envisioned Anglican practices and beliefs as informing a way of life, a kind of faithful living into faithful dying. We have portrayed that way of life as a theological and ethical journey in which we Christians not only pursue well-marked trails, but also blaze new paths, guided by our common faith, oriented as it is in God. As the task force neared the end of our work, we realized that the metaphors of "a way of life" and "a moral and theological journey" characterized not only the Anglican vision that we had presented but our own working endeavors as well. Now we step back to assess where we have been, how we arrived at the end, and in what ways the path that we have walked might serve others in the Church who address difficult moral issues.

The task force was called together for a clear purpose: to study the theological and ethical implications of issues that arise for Christians approaching death. We began our exploration of the contemporary realities of the world of health care at the end of life with a map whose main path had been set out by the Christian faith as seen through the distinctive prism of the Anglican tradition. We soon found that this path led into uncharted areas.

This caused us some concern. How could task force members, who in our usual courses of work took somewhat different approaches to resolving difficult issues, find a satisfactory method of proceeding? How could we, with varying stances on how to address troubling end-of-life issues, find common ground on which to tread? We took courage from our mutual commitment to the Christian faith as it has been shaped by the Anglican tradition. We also derived strength and new insights from many Episcopalians, both clergy and laypersons, who responded to our request for comments, ideas, and materials related to Christian care near the end of life.

As we moved forward, we came to realize that we were engaging in a process of theological and moral discernment akin to the one we set out in Part I of this volume. This process can perhaps best be characterized as a faithful, respectful conversation, in which, over and over again, we returned to the theological bases of our thought and the ethical imperatives of our beliefs. In this process, we listened to voices that enlarged our sense of the complex and painful human realities of fear, hope, and grief that those near the end of life face today. We entered deeply into the riches of the Anglican tradition and into dialogue with contemporary voices within the Church. We listened to those who provided insights into how the Church has and has not made provision, ethically, spiritually, and practically, for those approaching death and those caring for them.

Such conversation, we came to realize, is a central work of the Church. The Church is the voice that seeks to bear witness to God in the world, inviting us to live into God in our dying as in our living. This witness and ministry of the Church can be born only where conversations are opened and deepened between those who are dying, those who care for them, and the living, historical reality we call the Church.

From these conversations, we have sought to offer something of the wisdom and resources that our rich theological, ethical, and liturgical tradition offers us as Christians at the beginning of the twenty-first century. In turn, this has led us to some modest but concrete conclusions about what needs to be done and not done, by Christians and by a society, for those near the end of life. We bring these conclusions together here, addressing them to four distinct, and yet sometimes overlapping, groups: individuals, families, friends, and healthcare professionals; congregations; the church-at-large; and public policy makers.

FOR INDIVIDUALS, FAMILIES, FRIENDS, AND HEALTHCARE PROFESSIONALS

• *The use and misuse of medical technology in those near the end of life.* We are called as Christians to use medical technology in ways that honor the whole person in the unity of body and soul and thus the ends and purposes of human life. We are called to sustain life as long as persons deem this fitting and appropriate as they seek to live out their lives in light of such shared values as love, justice, loyalty, and beneficence. This means that we are not required to continue medical treatment when it creates suffering and places burdens upon those approaching death that do not serve human good and the ends and purposes of life.

• *The use and misuse of artificial nutrition and hydration in those near the end of life.* Artificial nutrition and hydration are forms of medical treatment that are qualitatively different from ordinary feeding. There is a moral presumption that they should be used for persons who are seriously ill and approaching death. However, they should be declined or ended when their use would be disproportionately burdensome or futile and would deny such values as love, justice, loyalty, and beneficence, as these reflect the ends and purposes of human life.

• *Providing appropriate pain relief for those near the end of life.* Those near death should be provided with appropriate pain relief by healthcare professionals. When the relief of pain and suffering in dying persons requires the use of narcotic doses that could hasten death, it is morally and legally appropriate to provide these drugs in order to alleviate suffering, but not with the intent of causing death. The use of pain-relieving drugs that may result in total sedation can also be appropriate at this time. The fear of addiction in dying patients who receive pain-relieving drugs is misplaced; addiction in such persons is rare.

• *Refraining from physician-assisted suicide near the end of life.* Physician-assisted suicide, in which a physician gives a patient a drug or other medical means of ending life, is not to be confused with withdrawing burdensome or futile life-sustaining treatment near the end of life. Members of the task force believe that the Episcopal Church should continue to oppose physician-assisted suicide near the end of life for several reasons. Suicide is never just a private, self-regarding act. It denies our relationship of love and trust in God and sets ourselves up as gods in the place of God. It also denies the dependence we all have upon others as members of the community and so denies others the sense of meaning and purpose they can derive from caring for us as we approach death. Physician-assisted suicide would erode our trust in physicians who are pledged to an ethic of healing. It would also have a damaging social impact on those in our society who are the most vulnerable. Society and the dying themselves could come to think that they should die because they are burden upon others. The practice of physician-assisted suicide not only departs from the teaching of the Christian tradition, but is also unnecessary, given our ability to provide palliative care to those near death.

• *Telling the truth within the health professional–patient relationship.* Respect for persons as bound in community with others and as bearing the right and responsibility to make treatment choices means that health professionals should provide patients with accurate information about their condition. There are important issues of timing and wording, as well as differences in cultural emphases, that caregivers should take into account in disclosing the truth to patients.

• *Uses of advance directives for treatment near the end of life.* It is appropriate for Christians to prepare advance directives, including "living wills" and durable powers of attorney for health care, to direct their care near the end of life. Although both forms of advance directive have certain limitations as a way of responding to issues that arise near the end of life, they provide a concrete way in which to promote advance planning, communication, and interaction between a person and those close to him or her. Practically, they prepare others to act on our behalf as we approach death.

• *Care of those with limited decision-making capacity.* Adults who have never had the capacity to make their own treatment decisions or who have had this capacity only intermittently should be cared for in light of what those close to them perceive as their good, needs, interests, and concerns. As for all persons, there is no Christian obligation to continue treatment of those who cannot make decisions for themselves when that treatment fails to offer a reasonable chance of recovery or causes suffering that burdens the ability to continue in the larger purposes of life. Although children cannot provide fully informed consent for refusing, beginning, continuing, or ending their treatment, it is important to have them share in the decision-making process in order that they may assent, given their capacity, to treatment decisions, especially those made near the end of life. As children mature, their wishes should be given increasing weight in the decision-making process.

FOR CONGREGATIONS

• *Congregational measures that can help us accept our mortality.* Congregations must be unafraid to speak of death. They can help us to cut through our denial of death in several specific ways. Clergy can explore the subject of dying in preaching and in teaching. Parishes can offer presentations about issues near the end of life at adult forums and other educational offerings. A developing *ars moriendi,* or art of dying, literature circulating among parishes around the country can provide assistance to those within congregations who are concerned about coping with end-of-life matters for themselves and for those they love.

• *Sustaining a community of care within the congregation for those near death.* The congregation can act in many ways to alleviate the fear of abandonment of those within and outside the parish who are near death. Within the parish community, clergy can encourage private prayer for the sick and dying. They can also make known the resources in *The Book of Common Prayer* for those approaching the end of life. As part of parish life, visitations of the sick, healing ministries, programs of respite care for families and of assistance with household chores can all be provided. Congregations can also assist in the development and support of local hospices.

• *Congregational programs to care for those who mourn.* Congregations are called to encourage members to visit those who are bereaved and to develop programs of visitation and support that extend well beyond the few months after death. Grief support groups sponsored by churches have been immensely helpful to those who mourn. Some congregations have created memorial gardens or columbariums where the ashes of those who have died can be buried. Memorial gardens or columbariums offer the sense of the connection of the living and the dead who are bound together as one church in union with God.

FOR THE CHURCH-AT-LARGE

• *Offering ordained and lay ministers greater preparation for addressing end-of-life matters.* Contemporary realities of ministering to the dying call ministers into changing social situations that are fraught with novel ethical, theological, and pastoral issues. New and expanded educational resources that explore such areas as medical ethics, ministry to the dying, and theological questions related to the end of life need to be developed through seminaries, continuing education courses, diocesan meetings, clergy retreats, and other clergy gatherings. End-of-life care is not a "special interest" within the ministry but a central one, since all of us will die and will need the prayers and support of the community of faith at that time.

• *Expanding liturgical resources for those ministering to persons near the end of life.* In a society characterized by "the ritual incompetence of mourners," secular liturgies are being created to address the unmet needs of those who die within healthcare institutions, as well as the needs of their families and friends. Within the Church, new rituals are also beginning to spring up in response to a cry for ritual support near the end of life. The Church is called not only to use available rituals for those near the end of life but also to expand them and to develop new services and prayers. These should be directed toward the needs of individuals who learn they are terminally ill, those who make a decision to withdraw life-sustaining treatment, and those who have begun to receive hospice care.

• *Developing an association of Episcopal healthcare groups and individuals involved in healthcare policy.* Episcopal Church groups involved in health care, such as Episcopal healthcare organizations, the National Episcopal Health Ministries, and the Assembly of Episcopal Healthcare Chaplains, as well as individuals who develop or teach about health policy, should be drawn together in an association. This body would communicate to policy makers and to the public the positions of the Episcopal Church regarding healthcare policy, especially as they affect those approaching the end of life. This association would also be responsible for advocating for a healthcare system that would guarantee decent and appropriate primary care for all, keeping abreast of the rapidly changing healthcare market and developments in biomedical research, and collecting and developing resources and teaching materials related to access to health care for the use of dioceses, congregations, and individuals.

FOR PUBLIC POLICY MAKERS

• *Providing hospice care for those who are "terminally ill" and for those in the advanced stages of chronic illness.* The spiritual imperative to provide comfort care for those approaching death leads us to call upon legislators and public policy makers to make more adequate and comprehensive palliative care available for those eligible for hospice care. We ask them to remove existing legal and regulatory obstacles to the provision of adequate pain management and palliative care, especially to those near death and to enable timely referrals to hospice for patients eligible for this form of care. Finally, we call upon legislators and public policy makers to promote the development of appropriate care grounded in the model of hospice care for those in the advanced stages of chronic illness who are not eligible for hospice care but for whom death is expected in the foreseeable future.

• *Rejecting physician-assisted suicide as a matter of public policy.* To sanction physician-assisted suicide as a matter of public policy would undercut the sense of the primary importance of human life that is essential to continued respect and care for human life in our society. Such a policy might well lead to a social climate in which the old, sick, and disabled would be pressured into killing themselves to avoid being a burden upon others. We do not support the cruel extension of suffering at the end of life but call instead for the provision of adequate and appropriate palliative care for those approaching death. Furthermore, we unequivocally and militantly insist that the practices, financing patterns, and habits that allow miserable dying to continue within this country and elsewhere must be changed.

When the task force reflected at its final meeting on the process through which it had come to these conclusions, we were poignantly aware of the spirit of cooperation that had grown up among us. We remarked that our experience in working together had been unlike any we had experienced before in a working group. This was, in large part, because we were not narrowly focused on the details of particular rights and wrongs or on the specifics of public policy. Rather, our primary concern was to articulate how the Christian faith informs our responses to end-of-life issues because it offers a deeper, broader perspective—not one of problem-solving but of how we may live more fully in the presence of God in our dying as in our living. In this sense, our focus has been on the journey of faith and the community that bears us forward in that journey, the Church. Above all, we take away from our deliberations the piercing conviction that facing up to death and dying is profoundly connected to how we live our lives as individuals and in community with one another. This same conviction is expressed by Paul in his letter to the Romans:

> We do not live to ourselves, and we do not die to ourselves. If we live, we live to the Lord, and if we die, we die to the Lord; so then, whether we live or whether we die, we are the Lord's. (Romans 14:7)

APPENDIX

For a list of organizational resources for those near the end of life and those close to them, see Appendix D in Committee on Medical Ethics, Episcopal Diocese of Washington, *Toward a Good Christian Death: Crucial Treatment Choices* (Harrisburg, Pa.: Morehouse, 1999), 132–134.

APPENDIX I. LAST THINGS: A PARISH RESOURCE FOR THE TIME OF DEATH

St. Matthias Episcopal Church, Waukesha, Wisconsin

CONTENTS

Saint Matthias Episcopal Church
111 East Main Street
P. O. Box 824
Waukesha, Wisconsin 53187-0824
(262) 547-4838
FAX: (262) 547-465

FOREWORD

Grace and peace be with you in the Risen Christ!
What follows on these pages does not represent an original effort. We are deeply indebted to the ground-breaking work done by St. Thomas' Episcopal Church in Cincinnati (Terrace Park), Ohio, and to subsequent revisions prepared by Calvary Episcopal Church in Cincinnati (Clifton), Ohio; Christ Episcopal Church in Cape Girardeau, Missouri; St. Paul's Episcopal Church in Pittsburgh (Mt. Lebanon), Pennsylvania; Christ Church Cathedral in Cincinnati; and to Rev. Charles F. Brumbaugh, Rector, The Church of Ascension & Holy Trinity. We have edited and adapted these booklets to the customs of St. Matthias Episcopal Church and its surrounding communities.

We are also grateful to the many people who have made this current revision possible by sharing their wisdom and experience, particularly Mary Botsford, parish nurse; Nancy Cole, Episcopal Church Women; Becky Huppert, Altar Guild; Robbi Heighway, music director; Betty Loth, secretary; Florence Melster; Memorial and Columbarium Committees; the Rev. Joanne Skidmore; Eleanor Timberlake, Flower Guild; and John Trotter, Endowment Fund chair.

Faithfully,

The Rev. Dr. Douglas Sparks
Serving as Rector and Pastor
Saint Matthias Episcopal Church
Ordinary Time 1999

INTRODUCTION

Death is one of the few things of which we can be certain. And yet, in spite of its inevitability, the time of death—our own or the death of a loved one—is always a time of crisis. The intensity of the crisis will often vary depending upon the age of the one who has died, the suddenness of that death, the suffering involved, and how close we are to the person. But a critical variable is how prepared we are to face death. Can we come to view death as the last act in the journey of life?

Unfortunately, in most aspects of our lives, we avoid the fact of death; therefore, in spite of its inevitability, we tend to come to death not only suffering with grief but also unprepared. Death then forces us to do what we don't want to do and to make important decisions for which we have not carefully planned. As a result, the crisis deepens and becomes even more painful.

This booklet, intended for use by St. Matthias parishioners, begins with certain premises:

- Grieving is human, and the Church seeks to support mourners through this natural process.
- The more we consider the issues surrounding death and grief, the better we will be able to deal with the loss of a loved one, and to face death ourselves.
- Planning for our own death can ease the crisis for our survivors.
- The Christian faith speaks directly to us about death and grief.
- The rites and practices of death and burial ought to be both a comfort to survivors and a reflection of our understanding of death in the light of the Gospel of Jesus the Christ.
- We bear primary responsibility for ourselves—in both life and death.

The information in this booklet is written to help you reflect on and prepare for your own death and burial from the Episcopal Church. It should also be of value in aiding others with this process. In addition, the Burial Instruction Form can serve as a guide for planning a burial for which no advance preparations have been made. The clergy, staff, and parishioners of St. Matthias stand ready to assist in clarifying the contents of this booklet or in answering any questions that may arise from its use.

Grief

It is impossible, within the scope of this booklet, to deal in depth with all the psychological, social, and spiritual facets of grief. There are many fine books and pamphlets on the subject; if you would like to learn more, the St. Matthias clergy and our parish nurse can assist you in identifying materials and help you locate desired resources. The purpose of this section is to present reflections based on a review of the printed material and on personal experiences of grief and loss.

Grieving is a natural process that tends to follow a fairly predictable pattern. Knowing about these so-called stages of grief may be quite helpful—particularly in reassuring you that the intense, aching, up-and-down turmoil you are enduring is "normal." However, it is crucial to remember that, even though grief is a universal human experience, each one of us is affected by death differently and that each one of us moves through grief in our own way. There is no single, "cookie-cutter" pattern for mourning.

WHEN A LOVED ONE BECOMES TERMINALLY ILL

In the case of a prolonged terminal illness, the grieving process may begin long before death. In fact, when the family and the dying person are able to share what is happening, they are often able to move through various aspects of grief together. This can lead to a more peaceful death for the dying, greater comfort for the survivors, an enhanced ability to plan for the future, and a less complicated bereavement process for those who are left. Often the dying person can minister to others as much as they minister to him or her.

Preparing for death, spiritually and emotionally, reflecting upon one's life with family or caregivers, and managing pain are some of the key elements of hospice programs. When medically and physically possible, people may want to choose the home (home may also be places like nursing homes and group homes) or in-patient hospice as the place to die. Hospitals emphasize services where there is a need for acute care and hope for a cure. It is often difficult for the medical team to change the focus to palliative or supportive care for the person and family when little hope remains for survival.

Usually more comfortable and care-oriented, the hospice setting may be more conducive to ministering to and with the dying. Hospice care focuses on enhancing the person's comfort and improving that person's quality of life. Hospice believes in empowering the person and following the person's desires. Hospice affirms life and neither hastens nor postpones the end of life. There have been excellent advances in pain control, and hospice staff are experts in this field. Many people with terminal illnesses endure a great deal of pain and other symptoms that can be relieved or reduced with proper pain management.

Nonetheless, in our society, many deaths take place in a hospital. In that setting, communicating the needs and wishes of the person and family about death to physicians and hospital staff becomes essential. Discussions beforehand among family members, clarifying these issues, can be very helpful.

Individuals may want to draft a living will and/or a durable power of attorney for health care to ensure that their wishes are known and carried out. These documents can also take some of the burden off family members. Most family members will carry out your wishes if they are known. This is especially helpful when they are not the wishes of other family members or when family members disagree. Without direction from the patient and family, the hospital staff may be required to initiate or continue treatment that is costly and of no benefit to the dying patient. The St. Matthias clergy and parish nurse are available to assist with prayerful consideration of these difficult matters.

Beyond the major decisions, patients and families should also express their needs for privacy, exceptions to visiting rules, and any other wishes that will aid the person and family as they move through the dying and live in both the grieving and celebrating of life shared and lost.

THE GRIEVING PROCESS

Whether grieving begins before death or after, it is the normal process of personal adjustment to the loss of a significant person. It is a natural part of one's life.

Grieving helps us: (1) deal with the reality of our feelings toward the person who has died and the loss of that person; (2) grow toward acceptance of the death; (3) search for meaning in the death and for our own life; (4) become reintegrated into our communities; and (5) begin to move on with our life.

When someone around whom our lives found meaning is gone, we typically experience a whole host of feelings: shock, numbness, sadness, depression, guilt, regret, anger, loneliness, anxiety, dread, relief, apathy, physical symptoms of stress, combinations of any of these, and many others. These feelings aren't "good" or "bad"—they just *are*. And they must be faced. Talking and crying, especially in the supportive company of persons who care about us, is a significant way of getting in touch with our feelings and often brings some comfort and release. We may feel like we're on a roller coaster with our feelings. One day or moment may be good, followed by a very low day. This is normal.

After the initial shock, people often tend toward avoidance and denial. What we say or don't say, our preoccupation with details, and even our displays of emotion are often designed to buffer ourselves from the painful yet unyielding reality of the death.

All the while, we find ourselves compelled to delve deeper and grapple with questions of ultimate meaning. Human beings are creatures who ponder our purpose in life and our destiny in death. The burial and the rites of the Church can be profoundly helpful in sorting out these significant issues. They are a recognition that we are part of a community of faith that assists us in the healing process. Discussion and counseling can also help.

As time passes and we begin to accept the fact of death in the depths of our being, we discover—in spite of the occasional setback—that we are indeed beginning to heal and to move on.

A key transition takes place as we gradually return to our usual rhythms of church, work, education, and recreation and become reintegrated into our communities. Often, we will not feel like doing this. We will question whether our old routines are worth the effort. And we will feel like retreating and turning in upon ourselves.

This is perhaps most evident when a spouse dies and we are no longer a "couple" but a "single," and we feel uncomfortable in that new role. It is not unusual for widows and widowers to feel unwelcome. But, more often than not, this is simply a reflection of our own grief and of the discomfort of others who truly *want* to help but just don't know *how*.

Of course, getting on with our lives doesn't mean immersing ourselves in frenzied activity for the sake of "keeping busy," nor does it mean forcing ourselves into making hasty decisions on important matters (e.g., selling a home or changing jobs). In fact, most experts recommend waiting six months to a year before making these types of major decisions if at all possible. But as we gently return to our customary activities and to those associations and relationships that have given our life pleasure and meaning, we find that—although our lives have been changed forever—we are, indeed, able to cope.

To grieve is to feel and to reflect, to hold on and to let go, to remember and to move on. We must do it ourselves. But there are friends, associates, church members, support groups, clergy, and professionals who stand ready to help us work through the ache of loss. Above all, there is God, who is with us in the midst of our suffering and struggles. Personal prayer and worship with your parish family can be an enormous source of strength and sustenance. The clergy and parish nurse are available to help those who are grieving to explore what support they need and help them make connections for that support.

CHILDREN AND GRIEF

One of the most difficult problems for families is helping children through the crisis of death. Adults have an understandable, natural desire to shield children from the shock, sadness, and pain of grief. When death comes, however, children, like adults, need the opportunity to deal with the hard reality of their loss and their turbulent feelings of grief.

Ideally, adults can help children begin to understand death long before it comes as a family crisis. Even young children see and hear about death on television, in stories, in nature, when a funeral procession passes by, when a pet dies. In these moments, open and honest communication with someone they trust can help children begin to accept death as a natural part of life and to learn reliable, helpful information.

When someone close dies, children should be told and allowed to participate in the process of grief. This does not mean forcing the child, but allowing the child to search, see, hear, question, and talk. Children experience the same range of emotions as adults and should be encouraged to express those feelings in words, crying, play, songs, drawings, and questions. Adults should allow children to see them cry and acknowledge their own sadness.

Including even young children in the rituals at the time of death is appropriate. While the decision about how children will participate is a family judgment, it does seem that children often benefit from being included in some way.

The child's feeling of exclusion and fantasies about death may be more difficult and frightening than actually seeing, knowing, and being a part of the family in saying good-bye. It is very helpful to explain in advance what the child can expect to see, hear, and do.

Children tend to have very concrete questions about death. They also tend to take our words literally. Adults should use language carefully, providing clear, simple explanations. (For example, to speak of the dead person as "asleep" is confusing and may even make a child afraid to fall asleep. To say that God "took" someone because "God needed her or him more" can make a child wonder about the goodness of God and can make the child angry because he or she still needs the person who died.) Rather than anticipating what a child might say or ask, listen carefully for what the child's thoughts, ideas, and concerns are. Children may need to ask questions again and again.

The most helpful response to the grieving child's needs is warm reassurance from a caring adult. We can convey to children our faith in the loving presence of God, who cares for the departed and who will continue to care for us through the hands and hearts of his people.

Adolescents especially need peer support as they struggle with death and dying issues. Be attentive to the adolescent's relationships and work to see that he or she has friends that remain faithful through the challenge. There are also support groups that bring together children or adolescents in similar circumstances. Again, the St. Matthias clergy and parish nurse are available to assist with identifying and connecting with these types of groups.

HOW TO BE A HELPFUL VISITOR

How can we help care for those who have suffered the loss of a loved one? This is a challenge—sometimes because we are uncomfortable with death itself, sometimes because we don't know the state of mind of the family (and occasionally don't even know the family), and sometimes because we simply don't know what to do or say.

Here are several suggestions. First and foremost, don't be afraid to intrude! Mourners often feel terribly isolated; these feelings are exacerbated if family and friends, feeling awkward and unsure, avoid them. A good rule of thumb is simply this: *Be there; be yourself.* There is not always a need to do or say anything. The fact that you cared enough to be present is itself a precious gift.

However, if the bereaved seem ready and willing to open up and talk about their concerns, be prepared to listen. You don't have to supply any profound answers. Just thank God that these people trust you enough to share their feelings and needs with you. And know that in your companionship and conversation, God is truly present and bringing his healing Spirit to bear.

If you feel moved to speak, express what you are thinking and feeling about the deceased out of your own experience—if this can be done without laying a greater burden on the family. (Remember: the grieving family doesn't need to minister to *you* as well as to themselves!) One caveat: it is not wise to say, "I know how you feel." You may not.

Take the initiative and ask about the needs of the bereaved. What you learn from them and from your own observations can guide you into meaningful and practical assistance for the family.

Finally, call on the bereaved one month, three months, even a year after the death. Holidays, anniversaries, and other special occasions can be especially difficult times for those who mourn. It is often well after the crowds have melted away that our friends are in the greatest need.

DO'S TO BEING A COMFORTER

• Be present. Mourners often feel terribly isolated. There is not always a need to do or say anything. The fact you cared enough to be present is itself a precious gift.
• Be an active listener. Focus on the grieving person's feelings. Avoid focusing on your own feelings and having the bereaved comfort you.
• Make every effort to offer specific support. Statements such as "May I bring dinner over on Friday?" or "May we have the children over to play on Thursday?" are more helpful than saying "Is there anything I can do for you?" In all likelihood, the bereaved doesn't know how you can help.
• While you may have been through something similar, it is never the same. Avoid telling someone, "I know how you feel," as we really don't know how someone feels in these times. Some may experience great grief immediately, others may be feeling numbness, others may be experiencing relief that the person is no longer suffering, some may be feeling guilt for things done or said and things left undone or unsaid, and some will feel all these things jumbled up. There may be a time much later to share and support our mutuality in loss and grief, but this is not the time.
• Remember to stay in contact in the weeks or months after the funeral. It gets very lonely after the crowds fade away.
• Encourage the sharing of stories that involved the one who has died. There are times it may seem as if the person who has died didn't exist or has been forgotten. You can help keep the memory alive by encouraging these stories. If you do this, be an active listener as well, watching and listening for the bereaved's reactions.
• As uncomfortable as it may feel, be willing to be with the bereaved in their tears. You don't need to fix the pain or stop the tears. Just sit with them as they grieve.
• Remember that birthdays, anniversaries, holidays, and other special occasions can be very difficult times for those who mourn.
• Pray for the family, and pray with the family if they are comfortable with that. Know that in your companionship and conversation, God is truly present and bringing his healing Spirit to support and surround you with God's love.

A CHRISTIAN PERSPECTIVE ON DEATH

Christians experience what every human being feels and needs when confronting death. The Christian faith does not deny the hard reality of death, nor does it shield us from the pain of grief. But our faith can make a significant difference in how we view death and cope with loss.

For Christians, the decisive event of human history is Easter: the death and Resurrection of Jesus the Christ. This is *God's* story, but it is *our* story too. We are "Easter people" because we believe that "when we had fallen into sin and become subject to evil and death," God, in his infinite love for us, sent Jesus, his only Son, "to share our human nature, to live and die as one of us, to reconcile us to [himself], the God and Father of all" (BCP, 362).

Yes, like Jesus, we shall die, But, also like Jesus, we shall be raised to newness of life! "For to your faithful people, O Lord, life is changed, not ended" (BCP, 382). Therefore, our assurance as Christians is that nothing, not even death, shall separate us from the love of God in Christ Jesus our Lord (Romans 6:3–5, 8:38–39; 1 Corinthians 15).

As Christians, then, we can talk about death openly and plan for it with both confidence and care. As Christians, our liturgies should be a celebration of that life, as well as a source of comfort and healing for the living.

PLANNING FOR DEATH

The crisis of death in a family forces sudden, complicated, and far-reaching decisions on those who are now responsible for arrangements. We are faced with a bewildering array of options at a time when we may be least capable of making appropriate decisions. Sometimes, differences of opinion arise within the family that, although understandable, add an extra burden to the already difficult situation. Because of these possibilities, most decisions concerning our death and burial should not wait until the time of death. The more planning we are able to accomplish *beforehand,* the sounder will be the decisions, and the more sparing and considerate we will be to those we leave behind.

The rights and desires we wish to exercise in death that express our beliefs and values should be clearly articulated not only to our next of kin but to all who may be affected by the choices we make.

The rest of this booklet concerns the most important elements of this planning. In it you will find discussion of various options concerning the burial of the body, the rites of the Church, stewardship in death, and other resources. Included is a Burial Instruction Form that can serve as a guide for consideration, discussion, and planning. Remember: the St. Matthias clergy and parish nurse stand ready to help you plan and to discuss your desires with others (including those who may find the subject painful or uncomfortable).

Ideally, we would recommend to you the following steps:
• Begin the process of planning now. Examine the contents of this booklet. Discuss your desires with your family. If you wish, discuss any questions/concerns with clergy.
• Complete the Burial Instruction Form. Ask your spouse and other family members to complete one too.
• Keep a copy of this form in a conspicuous place in your household. Give a copy to the parish office, and give other copies to your nearest of kin and other persons who will be overseeing your funeral arrangements (lawyer, funeral director, and so on). Ask for their reactions; they may have important concerns and perspectives to share. Amend the form as necessary.

• If you wish, make prefuneral arrangements with a funeral home and a cemetery.

• When death nears for you or a loved one, notify your parish family so that the Sacraments and other ministries of the Church may be provided.

• When the death of a loved one has occurred, notify the clergy, the attending physician, and then the funeral director.

The Church is a supportive and healing community, ready at all times to support those closest to the departed. We have been made one in Christ; it is our privilege to share one another's burdens.

Burial Practices

First, we shall discuss the two primary options for disposition of the body to be considered at the time of death: whole-body burial and cremation.

WHOLE-BODY BURIAL

When we talk about whole-body burial, we must consider many aspects.

Embalming. Most people think of embalming as an automatic part of whole-body burial, but it is not. However, for reasons related to health and decay, funeral homes generally encourage embalming whenever: (1) there will be an open-coffin viewing of the body over a period of several days or (2) a significant period of time will elapse between death and disposal of the body. Embalming is not needed when: (1) cremation immediately follows death, (2) burial immediately follows death ("direct burial"), (3) the body is refrigerated (most funeral homes, however, are not equipped for this), or (4) the body is immediately placed in a hermetically sealed coffin, which remains closed thereafter.

Coffins. Coffins come in a wide variety of materials, designs, and costs. The purpose of the coffin is to serve as a convenient receptacle for the body during the funeral and for burial. The purpose of the burial is to return the body to the elements, a process that should not be impeded unnecessarily. Therefore, spending great sums on a coffin designed to preserve the body is not recommended.

When the coffin is brought to the church, it is covered with a pall, which is a white cloth emblazoned with a cross. The white pall symbolizes our baptismal garment and the care and saving love with which God enfolds us. It also proclaims that, regardless of one's station in life, we are equal in the sight of God and so are buried equally. While the coffin is in the church, only the white pall will be used. If the family of the deceased desires to have the U.S. flag or some other draping, the appropriate place for that is at the burial site. We are redeemed through God's grace alone, hence, the funeral service is not about our accomplishments or our membership in organizations. The service is about our baptism into the life and death of our Savior and the Good News of God with us through Jesus Christ and the Holy Spirit.

Vaults/Liners. Today, most cemeteries require that coffins be placed in a vault or a grave liner, which is a container made of metal or concrete. The purpose of the vault is to prevent the ground from collapsing as the coffin deteriorates (a maintenance problem for cemeteries). Vaults are constructed in different ways and at different costs; all will serve the stated purpose. The more expensive vaults are designed to retard deterioration of the coffin and body. Again, since this is contrary to the purpose of burial, an inexpensive vault is recommended.

Lying in State. If there is to be a whole-body burial or cremation after the funeral, the body will "lie in state" until the time of the funeral. There are several locations to be considered.

The most desired location available for members of St. Matthias is the nave of the church.

Once the body is brought into the church, the coffin is closed and covered with a pall. The lighted Paschal candle is placed nearby, witnessing to the everlasting life that is ours through baptism into the death and Resurrection of Christ. This choice may benefit both the family and visitors.

• There is no cost to pledging members for the use of the church; however, there are expenses related to specific services provided. Specific information can be obtained from the parish office. For nonpledging members, there is a fee for the use of the church. Again, the parish office can provide this information.

• The church, especially for Christians, provides a prayerful setting for family and visitors. *The Book of Common Prayer, The Hymnal 1982,* and other materials for prayer and reflection would be available.

• There are two important needs during the grieving process: to be with people for support and to be alone for reflection or tears. The parish hall and fellowship room (if available), with facilities nearby for preparing refreshments, provide places for fellowship. Here, people could gather freely to talk and share. But they could also choose to go into the stillness of the worship space to be quiet and to pray.

• The church is home for members of the parish family, and they will feel more comfortable there than in an unfamiliar setting.

Years ago, the body would often lie in state in the home. This is still an option, although few of our homes are large enough, and this choice may be a burden to the family. Another option is the funeral home, which has become the most frequent location.

Another question about lying in state concerns whether the coffin should be open or closed. There are different opinions on this subject. The open coffin seems to allow for greater identification with the deceased; the closed coffin seems to help people face the finality of death and begin looking to the future. A middle-ground alternative is to have a short open-coffin viewing for the family and close friends, and then to have it closed. Whichever alternative is chosen, at some point the coffin will be closed, and the family may want to witness the closing. (Remember: it is directed in *The Book of Common Prayer* that the coffin is closed when it is brought into the church, and it remains closed thereafter).

Grave Markers. Grave markers come in various sizes, shapes, and materials and can convey a variety of messages. Some cemeteries will prescribe or limit the type of grave marker allowed. Veterans have special markers available to them through the Veterans Administration. The type of marker, or whether there will be a marker at all, will be a matter of personal choice. It is good to remember that a simple marker will serve the purpose. Grave markers can, through symbols or inscriptions, bear witness to our faith in the Resurrection.

CREMATION

Cremation of the bodies of the deceased has long been an accepted practice in the Episcopal Church and the Anglican Communion.

People who choose cremation usually do so for one or more of the following reasons: (1) with burial costs rising, cremation may provide an economical alternative; (2) ashes (or "cremains"), which take up very little space, may be interred in a number of different ways and places; (3) cremation is often chosen when there is no need or desire to have a grave site to visit, either because there is no family or because the family will not be returning.

Cremations generally take place soon after death. All that is needed is the doctor's certificate of death. The coroner's approval is not necessary unless there is a special concern about the cause of death.

There are several options related to cremation. Cremation may take place either before or after the service. If before, then the body can be taken directly to the crematorium upon death; the service can then either be done without the ashes present or with the ashes when they are returned. If cremation is to take place after the funeral, you should be aware that the body is usually embalmed and placed in a coffin; in this case, there is a negligible cost advantage. Interment of the ashes can be done whenever the ashes are returned, regardless of whether cremation precedes or follows the service.

Some have questioned the theological propriety of cremation (as well as autopsies and the donation of bodies or organs) on the grounds that it is an assault on the human body and problematic in terms of the resurrection of the body. We believe that this should not be an impediment. Flesh and blood cannot inherit the kingdom of heaven, and the resurrected body spoken of in Holy Scripture is a "spiritual body" which God will give us (1 Corinthians 15). Cremation simply hastens the natural process of returning the body to the elements.

Even so, cremation is still for many an emotional issue that should be discussed fully with the family before final plans are made. Survivors may feel morally affronted by having to arrange for a cremation, especially if they were not aware of it ahead of time. Another issue is the value for mourners of having a physical presence of the deceased at the funeral, either a body or ashes. This is a matter of choice and sensitivity to the needs of survivors.

St. Matthias Columbarium. In April of 1996, after prayerful consideration, the vestry of St. Matthias gave its support and encouragement to the Memorial Committee to initiate a parish columbarium. A columbarium was designed, crafted, and placed in the chapel. It will hold 140 niches. This columbarium is a visible sign of the Church's understanding of the Communion of Saints. It provides a natural repository and final resting place for the cremated remains of deceased baptized members of St. Matthias and their immediate family members. The current cost of each niche is $400, which includes the cost of engraving the name, date of birth, and date of death of each member. The engraving style will be determined by the church to ensure uniformity. There are no other costs.

Following the services for the Burial of the Dead, the ashes, enclosed in a simple urn that fits into the niche, are brought to the columbarium and the Committal is read from *The Book of Common Prayer*. The urn is then placed in the niche and the face plate is fastened. It is not possible to place flowers on the columbarium; however, flowers in memory of persons interred in the columbarium may be placed in the church or chapel, after consultation with the rector or assisting priest and the flower guild chair.

Please call the church office for information concerning burial details.

AUTOPSY

Especially in a hospital setting, the family may be approached at the time of death to consider allowing an autopsy of the deceased. Autopsies may answer questions asked by physicians and family members when the cause of death is not clear. Medical implications of hereditary diseases or conditions for other family members may also be learned from an autopsy. Physicians and scientists benefit from general medical knowledge gained from autopsies, and that knowledge may contribute to medical progress. In a few instances, an autopsy may be required by law under the jurisdiction of the coroner. Autopsies are performed with respect for the dignity of the human body. And an autopsy should not interfere with an open-coffin viewing or delay the funeral arrangements significantly. However, strong personal feelings or wishes about autopsy should be communicated in advance to assist the family's decision making.

ORGAN AND TISSUE DONATION

Advances in the field of transplantation allow the gift of organs and tissues at the time of death to offer significant benefits to those waiting for a transplant. Organs such as kidneys, liver, heart, and lungs may be donated. Donated corneas can be used to restore sight, and other tissues such as bone and skin can be used to help a patient's healing process.

Those wishing to be organ and tissue donors can indicate this on their driver's license or by carrying a Uniform Donor Card with them at all times. It is crucial to communicate the intention to donate organs and tissue to the next of kin who may be consulted by the medical staff about organ donation at the time of death. So that organs and tissue may be of the most benefit, the donation procedure is performed immediately after death. The body may then be buried or cremated.

Donating organs can be a profound gift of love for those who benefit from the gift and their loved ones. It can also provide comfort for the bereaved, a real sense that giving of ourselves continues even into death. It is important to consider prayerfully what you would like done and communicate your decision to your family and doctor. "Don't take your organs to heaven; heaven knows we need them here."

DONATION OF THE BODY FOR RESEARCH

Bodies may be given to medical schools for use in training medical personnel and for other research. Specific arrangements for this should be made in advance with a medical school. When a person dies, the school will accept the body if they have need of it and if it has not been severely damaged. The body may be transported directly to the medical school, or, if there is to be a funeral first, the body will be embalmed. The school will often pay for transportation to the school and for cremation when they have finished with it, and either bury the ashes or return them to the family, depending on the family's wishes.

There are positive aspects to this form of disposal of the body. We do suggest, however, that this option be discussed explicitly with one's family before arrangements are made, so that they may be prepared for this action. We would also recommend consideration of how important it will be for the family to have a physical presence of the body as a factor in their mourning; they can then decide whether the body should be given before or after the funeral, or indeed at all. Furthermore, the donor and the family are urged to consult an attorney and their funeral director to be advised of any laws or regulations pertaining to the donation of the body for research.

VISITATIONS

At some point there will probably be a desire to have a time of visitation to allow people to share this moment with one another. The same three options of home, church, and funeral home remain. Again, the home may be the most comfortable setting. And the church still has the advantage of providing both a place for sharing and a place for prayer.

How much time to set aside for visitation is a personal matter. There are times family members take on a host or hostess role at lengthy visitations, which can be very difficult. You can help by having some close friends identified to serve as host or hostess. Visitation is by no means mandatory and should be the decision of the family.

FUNERAL DIRECTORS

For most burials, after the rector of St. Matthias has been notified, the services of a funeral director will be sought. There are many details that need to be attended to at the time of death that the family has neither the time nor the energy to accomplish, and the funeral director will do these things efficiently.

To make the best use of funeral directors, it is necessary to have in mind what you want to happen. This is where preplanning a burial can be of immense importance. If you know what you want, funeral directors will be delighted to help you accomplish your purposes. If you don't know what you want, they will help you make decisions.

But remember that, contrary to what the title "funeral director" seems to imply, the *family* (in consultation with the funeral director and with help and guidance from the rector or assisting priest) is the ultimate decision maker concerning disposal of the body and other burial decisions, and the *church* (in consultation with the family) is in charge of the funeral services.

Funeral directors will itemize in full the costs of their services and provide only those services the family requests. It is quite proper to discuss costs and services anticipated from the funeral home.

The Rites of Burial

The liturgy for the dead is an Easter liturgy.
It finds all its meaning in the resurrection. (BCP, 507)

At the center of burial practices are the rites of the Church. These rites:
• are the acts wherein we dispose of the body of our loved ones;
• focus our attention on the reality of death, and help us sever the relationships that exist in this life;
• are the means of allowing the community to recognize the loss of its members;
• offer the members of the community an opportunity to support the families and one another;
• provide mourners an opportunity to express their emotions in a supportive setting;
• give dignity and meaning to the end of life;
• provide an opportunity to express faith in the promises of the Gospel, and to bear witness to the loving presence of God in our midst.

The rites cannot fully accomplish these tasks, encompass all of the mourning, or express every thought and feeling present. But they do serve as the grace-filled means of drawing these together in focus so all may come away comforted and uplifted in the hope of the Resurrection. To be sure, mourning will continue, but the rites stand as a sign of the unity we share—both in mourning and in hope.

The rites of the Church are appropriate at three junctures in the passage from life into death:

1. The Church's ministry to the dying person and his or her family before the point of death
2. The funeral service in the church
3. The committal at the final resting place

PREFUNERAL SERVICES

Although such services are not strictly a part of the funeral, the Episcopal Church provides resources and suggestions for prayer, reflection, and worship prior to the Burial of the Dead.

When death is imminent, the family may be gathered. The clergy should be called in to minister both to the dying person and to the family. Holy Communion may be administered, if possible, and prayers offered with, and for, the dying person. The Sacraments of Penance/Reconciliation of a Penitent (BCP, 447) and Ministration to the Sick (BCP, 453) may also be administered. A priest, deacon, layperson, or member of the family may lead those gathered in prayer. A "Litany at the Time of Death" is provided for this purpose in *The Book of Common Prayer* (462–465). It is most appropriate for the dying person to participate, if possible, in the prayers.

After death has occurred, it may be desirable for family and friends to gather for prayer and reflection prior to the funeral. This might be a rather informal gathering with participants sharing their thoughts, feelings, and remembrances. The "Litany at the Time of Death" (BCP, 462) or "Prayers for a Vigil" (BCP, 465) might be used, along with the reading of Holy Scripture. These services may be led by clergy or laypersons.

Please remember: "The death of a member of the Church should be reported as soon as possible to, and arrangements for the funeral should be made in consultation with, the Minister of the Congregation" (BCP, 490).

THE FUNERAL LITURGY

The time of the service should be set so that most people who would want to be present can be. If the family wishes, the funeral may be held in the evening with interment (committal) earlier in the day, or even the following day.

"Baptized Christians are properly buried from the church" (BCP, 490). This is where they were baptized and began their journeys into eternal life. This is where they were nourished with Word and Sacrament. This is where they met in prayer and song, fellowship and service with other Christians And so this is where they should be brought as they enter upon their heavenly inheritance.

When the body is brought into the church, it is greeted by the celebrant and members of the altar guild. The celebrant may say prayers provided in *The Book of Common Prayer* (466–467) while the altar guild covers the coffin with the white pall. At the time of the funeral, the family and friends are seated in the nave. The service begins with a solemn procession to the chancel steps, where the coffin is placed near the Paschal candle.

The clergy plan the details of the funeral in consultation with the family. Remember: within the seemingly rigid format of the Prayer Book and Hymnal, there is a great deal of flexibility.

Readings. Suggested lessons and psalms are provided by the Prayer Book (470–480, 494–495). Other appropriate readings from Holy Scripture may be chosen instead. Members of the family or other laypersons may read the lessons, lead the Psalm, and/or lead the prayers of the people.

Homily. A funeral sermon is customarily preached by the clergy at St. Matthias. Generally this sermon: 1) gives thanks for the life and ministry of the departed, 2) proclaims the Gospel of hope in the Resurrection, 3) invokes prayer for the departed and those who grieve, 4) invites support for one another, and 5) encourages mourners to begin to move on with life.

A family member or friend may offer a reflective homily in addition to the homily, but as this is an extremely difficult task to take on in the midst of grief, great caution should be exercised in considering such a decision.

Music. Music can play a vital role in bearing witness to the Gospel. Instrumentals, solos, and choral anthems can speak of faith and hope through music as well as words. Perhaps the most meaningful option is the use of hymns sung by the entire congregation. Familiar, stirring hymns allow those gathered to praise God, bear witness to their faith, and express their emotions.

Easter hymns that proclaim the Resurrection are particularly appropriate. Family favorites that are faith-affirming may be chosen. The presider and/or the director of music would be pleased to assist you.

Suggested Hymns from *The Hymnal 1982*
178 *Alleluia, Alleluia*
199 *Come, Ye Faithful, Raise the Strain*
207 *Jesus Christ Is Risen Today*
208 *The Strife Is O'er*
287 *For All the Saints*
335 *I Am the Bread of Life*
379 *God Is Love, Let Heaven Adore Him*
388 *O Worship the King; All Glorious Above*
482 *Lord of All Hopefulness*
488 *Be Thou My Vision*
490 *I Want to Walk as a Child of the Light*
544 *Jesus Shall Reign*
618 *Ye Watchers and Ye Holy Ones*
637 *How Firm a Foundation*
645 *The King of Love My Shepherd Is*
662 *Abide with Me*
671 *Amazing Grace*
680 *O God, Our Help in Ages Past*
688 *A Mighty Fortress Is Our God*
691 *My Faith Looks Up to Thee*

There are alternative choices in our *Gather* and *Wonder, Love and Praise* hymnals.

Holy Communion. It is almost always appropriate to celebrate the Holy Communion during the Burial of the Dead. By God's grace, partaking of the body and blood of Jesus provides us with a foretaste of the kingdom of God, witnessing to the good news that we and all in the Communion of Saints are one in the Risen Christ.

However, if for some reason Communion is not appropriate, *The Book of Common Prayer* provides a Burial Office in either traditional (Rite One) or contemporary (Rite Two) language.

Flowers. St. Matthias provides a brochure outlining the placement of arrangements in the sanctuary and the nave of the church. The rector or assisting priest will go over this with the family representative or request that the person contact the chair of the flower guild. Flowers are not placed over the coffin or elsewhere in the sanctuary. Flowers sent by friends may be displayed in the narthex or the parish hall.

Worship Bulletins. A worship bulletin may be helpful, especially for those unfamiliar with the liturgy of the Episcopal Church. It also provides a keepsake for family and friends. St. Matthias will provide the worship bulletins.

Fees. Pledging members of St. Matthias Episcopal Church are not charged for the use of the church for the service or for having visitation or the body lying in state in the church. There are costs associated with the organist, sexton, and altar guild. For nonpledging members there is an additional fee for the use of the church. Contact the parish office for a current fee schedule.

Receptions. The family may want to greet friends in a place apart before or after the service. In this case, the Episcopal Church Women of St. Matthias would be pleased to provide cookies or cake along with beverages in the fellowship room or parish hall. (This may take the place of all or some of the preservice visitation.)

The church has committees established to offer these reception services. The funding comes from donations by church members. If the family desires additional food, they are welcome to arrange for that, in consultation with the reception committee.

THE COMMITTAL

The Committal is the last of the Church's burial rites, the final act of giving the body or ashes back to the elements, and of letting go. Thus, the grave or the St. Matthias Columbarium is the most appropriate site. The Committal service itself is a short one, consisting of opening anthems, words of committal, prayer, and dismissal. (The Committal may be said in the church if circumstances, such as inclement weather, make the grave site impractical. It may also be said before the service in the church, or prior to cremation.)

At the cemetery, the coffin is usually lowered into the vault, the vault is sealed, and the grave is filled after the family and friends have left. The family may choose to remain and witness this final act.

Ashes to be interred in the St. Matthias Columbarium are placed in the columbarium sometime after the funeral, using the rite of Committal in *The Book of Common Prayer*.

Ceremonies by fraternal or other groups are best conducted at the home, funeral home, or meeting place of the group rather than the church. If such groups want to have a grave-site ceremony, this should precede the Committal.

OTHER SERVICES OF THE CHURCH

There are a number of other opportunities for liturgies relating to death. If, for example, the burial of a loved one is to take place at such a distance that friends and family members are not able to attend, a separate memorial Eucharist might be celebrated. A second reason for an additional service might be a desire for the celebration of a memorial Eucharist before or after the funeral when, for whatever reason, the Holy Communion is not celebrated in the context of the funeral itself. Another wish might be to have a memorial service for the family and close friends somewhat later, in addition to the funeral. For example, after a particularly untimely or tragic death, the family may be somewhat more prepared to reflect and celebrate at a later date.

As you consider some of the issues and options presented in this booklet and begin to plan for your own burial, we suggest that you read through the burial rites in *The Book of Common Prayer* (462–507) in a reflective way. The Church's rites have both the purpose and flexibility to bring profound meaning to our passage into eternal life.

STEWARDSHIP IN DEATH

The earth is the LORD's and all that is in it. Psalm 24:1

The Minister of the congregation is directed to instruct the people, from time to time, about the duty of Christian parents to make prudent provision for the well-being of their families, and of all persons to make wills, while they are in health, arranging for the disposal of their temporal goods, not neglecting, if they are able, to leave bequests for religious and charitable uses. (BCP, 445)

It has been stated that your consideration of death gives rise to the need to plan ahead for this inevitable event. There are, however, two basic types of detailed planning involved in this process: (1) planning for the disposition and burial of your body, and (2) planning for the disposition of your estate (any money, property, or other assets that you will leave behind).

It is our hope that *both* types of planning will be informed by your faith in the Gospel of Jesus Christ. Estate planning is an essential aspect of Christian stewardship. As you prepare for your death, you will want to think about how you will want to share—to the glory of God and the ongoing care of God's people—the gifts God has graciously yet temporarily given into your possession.

The planning of your estate helps you to: (1) ensure financial security and adequate income during your life, and (2) leave the maximum amount to your heirs, including charities of your choice. To this end, a properly drawn will is essential! Without a legal will on file, state law will decide how your assets are to be distributed.

What follows are general ideas, not specific legal or tax advice. Laws that regulate giving are complex and constantly changing. *We strongly encourage you to seek your own competent legal and financial counsel on these matters.*

BEQUESTS TO SAINT MATTHIAS EPISCOPAL CHURCH

In your plans, we invite you to remember St. Matthias. For many of us, it is our spiritual home; God has richly blessed us and our loved ones through this parish family. But it is also good to remember that the church has a future without us, just as our families do.

The balance of this section suggests several methods for your consideration that can put St. Matthias in your estate plan. *Note: The St. Matthias Endowment Fund can provide you with more detailed information about the various available options.*

Wills. The most widely understood type of gift that is imbedded in your estate plan is a bequest by will benefiting St. Matthias' general operating budget and/or various special funds at your death. The federal government encourages such gifts by allowing an estate tax charitable deduction for gifts to qualified organizations. When mentioning St. Matthias, be sure to use its correct name and address, along with its tax identification number.

St. Matthias Memorial Fund. A wonderful way to give thanks for the life of a loved one is to make a contribution that will in some way continue to bless others. Gifts to the memorial fund are used to purchase items of lasting value for the church. Often many small gifts are accumulated in order that something needed in the life of the parish may be procured in the names of several deceased persons.

St. Matthias Endowment Fund. St. Matthias' ministry is supported primarily by the annual giving (pledges) of its members. The purpose of the endowment fund is to provide money for the maintenance and repair of church property and facilities. Gifts to the endowment fund are a wonderful way to support our church facilities. All moneys received are invested and the gains used to fulfill the fund's purpose. You may earmark your gifts as a memorial or special blessings, or to a specific use at the church; however, the vestry will have the final determination on spending each year.

St. Matthias has specific needs that require larger donations. Donating to the endowment fund ensures that these needs will continue to be met long after your bodily death.

Just as St. Paul urged the early Christians to set funds aside for work to be done by others, so giving to the endowment fund is a commitment to set aside funds to serve others in the future.

GENERAL NOTES REGARDING BEQUESTS

• *While you may specify how you want donations and memorials to be used, you are encouraged to have them unrestricted. We can never know what needs will arise in the future, and our church leaders and members need flexibility to grow the body of Christ as best for their times and not limited by what we find best for our times. The current policy of the vestry is that any unrestricted bequest is equally divided between the endowment fund and the memorial fund.*
• *It is also good to remember worthwhile ministries in the Episcopal Diocese of Milwaukee or the national Episcopal Church (such as the Presiding Bishop's Fund for World Relief).*

• *To guide others, it is helpful to list the designated memorials in both the obituary and the worship bulletin at the funeral.*

GIFTS OF ASSETS DURING LIFE

Gifts, direct or by bequest, can be given to St. Matthias in these forms: (1) cash, (2) appreciated securities, and (3) real property.

Any of these gifts may be "unrestricted" (the use to be determined by the vestry) or "restricted" (specified by the donor for a particular purpose, e.g., one of the special funds described above).

Note: It is important to remember that, in accordance with St. Matthias' Gift Policy, the vestry must expressly approve the acceptance of any restricted gift in order to ensure that the purpose envisioned for the gift is in harmony with the overall ministry and needs of the parish. Thus vestry approval should be secured before any restricted bequests are included in your will so you may be certain that your expectations can be fulfilled.

Cash. Generally, gifts of cash given during your lifetime are fully deductible for federal income tax purposes.

Appreciated Securities. If you hold securities that would have long-term capital gains tax consequences if sold, their outright gift to St. Matthias could mean a significant tax savings to you and would allow you to give an additional generous gift to St. Matthias.

Real Property. It is also possible for parishioners to make outright gifts to St. Matthias of a residence or other real estate, jewelry, antiques, or other valuable personal property.

Again, however, we strongly encourage you to consult with the rector and vestry (as well as with your attorney and/or financial advisor) about such gifts *before* making arrangements in order to determine whether or not the particular property can actually be accepted and used by St. Matthias.

PLANNED GIVING: GIFTS OF FUTURE INTEREST

It is not uncommon for families to hold assets that have appreciated in value, only to find themselves cash poor in day-by-day demands. It is still possible for such persons to expand their relationship to St. Matthias, to further the mission of the Church, and to expand their own current incomes by using one or more of these plans. Not only can they lower tax obligations, but in most cases they generate income for the donor and his or her heirs. Examples of these are (1) trusts and annuities, to benefit St. Matthias but with income to the donor, and (2) life insurance policies.

Trusts and Annuities. Laws designed to encourage gift support of nonprofit organizations make it possible to transfer cash or property into a charitable remainder trust that will:

• entitle you to a charitable deduction on your income tax;
• save long-term capital gains taxes you would have incurred had you sold the property;
• provide you or the lives of those you designate with income for life, subject to certain restrictions;
• preserve more of your estate for your heirs by reducing or eliminating federal estate taxes;
• give *you* greater control over assets that would ordinarily be lost to taxation;
• benefit St. Matthias after the deaths of those for whom income has been provided.

Life Insurance. Gifts of life insurance offer an opportunity to make a more substantial contribution to St. Matthias than you may dream possible. If an existing insurance policy is no longer needed for family protection, it may be given to St. Matthias. Alternately, the beneficiary can be changed to be St. Matthias. The value of a permanent policy at the time of the gift (i.e., the cash-surrender value) is deductible for federal income tax purposes. (If you continue to pay the premiums, those payments may also be deductible as charitable contributions. Furthermore, it is possible that, if a paid-up policy is given, the cost of purchasing a new, paid-up policy at your current age would be the value of the charitable contribution deduction.)

WHERE DO WE GO FROM HERE?

If you desire to give financially to St. Matthias upon your death, there are three things to do *now:*

1. If you are able to make a will and have not yet done so, ask your lawyer to prepare one for you, including a bequest for St. Matthias, or have your attorney amend your existing will. Instead of a bequest, you may wish to consider one of the trusts providing a life income, which are discussed above. You may want to decide how you want to earmark your gift, for what use, and if it is to be in memory of someone. If you wish to explore the various possibilities first, the St. Matthias clergy can direct you to members of the St. Matthias Episcopal Church Endowment Fund and other knowledgeable persons within the parish community.

2. Determine what, in cash or stock or other form, you might give now, totally apart from your will and your annual pledge, on a one-time gift basis.

3. Celebrate! Celebrate the abundance with which you have been blessed by God. Celebrate your generous support of our future. And share that joy with St. Matthias!

CONCLUDING REMARKS

We hope that you have now contemplated all or part of this booklet and that it finds a permanent and visible place among your household records.

Don't just file it away, however. In the short term, we ask that you take its recommendations and instructions to heart. Make a will. Consider filling out a living will and/or durable power of attorney for health care. Fill out the Burial Instruction Form to ensure that your wishes are known to your survivors and to your church.

In the long term, study and absorb the booklet's precepts. Contemplation of death now can lead you to steps that will deepen your faith and make the rest of your life richer and more meaningful.

Lastly, we bid you remember that God calls us to reverence him by the prudent stewardship of all that he has temporarily given into our care— our treasure, our talents, our very lives.

May this booklet be helpful as you, in your heart of hearts, come to grips with your "last things"!

APPENDIX 2. MEMORIAL GARDEN

St. Andrew's Episcopal Church, Saratoga, California

THE TRADITION

Saint Andrew's Memorial Garden has been provided as a place for burial of ashes of parishioners and their families.

As many visitors to old churches in England, Europe, and the eastern United States have learned, the churchyard has been a traditional place for the burial of the dead through centuries of Christian history. Only recently has Western society set aside separate areas for burial grounds, isolated and distant from the churches where the faithful worship.

Saint Andrew's space requirements and state law limit burial to ashes from cremation. Thus, the Memorial Garden is established to receive ashes, and the parish can return to the ancient custom of burying the dead on hallowed ground where generations of families will gather and worship.

HISTORY

Acting at the request of our vestry, a Memorial Garden Committee was founded in 1985 to provide a plan that would bring a memorial garden into being at Saint Andrew's.

The committee selected an approximately 700-square-foot area on the north side of the church, just outside the side door into the chapel.

The Memorial Garden is intended as a place of tranquility and natural beauty, set in the midst of the busy life of the parish. The garden is enclosed by a low, ornamental metal fence surrounding a lawn, bordered by native plantings, with a bench and area for meditation and rest.

BURIAL OF ASHES

Cremated remains of members of the parish and their families are interred in the garden and the cremated remains of others may be accepted at the

St. Andrew's Episcopal Church
13601 Saratoga Avenue
Post Office Box 2789
Saratoga, California 95070
(408) 867-3493

discretion of the rector. No markers are used and ashes are placed beneath the lawn area in biodegradable linen bags. A scale map indicates the location of individual ashes and is attached to the permanent burial records of the church, maintained in the clergy office.

A bronze memorial plaque placed on the wall just inside the chapel commemorates those buried in the garden.

It is acceptable to inter ashes that have been previously buried in other sites, from parish families and others at the discretion of the rector. Assistance in making arrangements for this relocation is available.

HOW IT HAPPENS

Arrangements for interment of ashes in the Memorial Garden are made in consultation with the rector, at which time the actual site selection is made. Burial sites may not be reserved in advance; however, once a family member's ashes have been interred, adjoining spaces may be held for spouses and children.

The cost for interring ashes in the Memorial Garden includes opening and closing the grave, providing the biodegradable linen bag, engraving a nameplate for the memorial plaque in the chapel, and helping to maintain the care of the garden with replacement plantings as necessary.

Flowers may be placed on the grave at any time. The sexton will remove them after their time has passed.

Interment services in the garden generally follow *The Book of Common Prayer* and are personalized by consultation between the rector and participants. Our use permit does not permit amplified sound.

The Memorial Garden is supervised by a Memorial Garden Committee nominated by the rector and appointed by the vestry. This committee provides the linen interment bags, supervises preparation for interment and engraving of memorial plates, and generally oversees the care and maintenance of the garden.

In acknowledging the Community of Saints,
the Episcopal Church counts both the living and the dead
among its members.
The community at Saint Andrew's may rejoice
that the Memorial Garden offers an opportunity for interment
on parish grounds.

APPENDIX 3. REGULATIONS AND CONDITIONS

St. Peter's Columbarium, Conway, Arkansas

The supervision of the use of and the maintenance of St. Peter's Columbarium and the allotment of crypts and units therein will be the responsibility of the vestry of St. Peter's Episcopal Church or its designee and will be governed by the following regulations and conditions:

1. The purchase price shall be established by contract between St. Peter's and Buyer. The purchase prices do not include the cost of interment, the cost of a plaque, or the cost of a marker. Additional charges relating to the cost of interment shall be charged for each use of an individual crypt.

2. At the time of purchase, Buyer shall, if feasible, designate the person (by name, not as a class) whose remains may be interred in an individual crypt. Each crypt is designed for one interment unless special request is made for multiple interments and approved by the Columbarium Board. The number of uses of the common crypt is unlimited, provided the required purchase prices are paid for each interment.

3. During his lifetime, from time to time, Buyer may change designation of the persons whose cremated remains may be interred, or Buyer may designate another in writing to exercise the right to specify others who may be interred in the crypt.

4. Buyers must be natural persons or the personal representative of a deceased or of an incompetent person. Two individuals may qualify as a Buyer, holding the right to use as joint tenants with right of survivorship, and not as tenants in common; those rights are exercisable jointly while both are living or by the survivor.

5. Except with the written consent of St. Peter's, Buyer's rights may not be assigned or transferred, and shall not be subject to claims of creditors. Buyer can be authorized to conduct the private sale of plot(s), but only with the written permission of the Columbarium Board. A transfer fee of $25.00 will be charged. Buyer's rights are no longer assignable after the first interment in a crypt.

6. A transfer fee of $25.00 shall be charged by St. Peter's should any existing Buyer be granted permission by the Columbarium Board to move his or her plot(s) to another location in the columbarium.

7. Cremated human remains only may be interred. Ashes may be deposited directly into the crypt or placed in a container that is

deposited in a crypt. The common crypt may accept only ashes deposited directly.

8. If a container is used, it must be of a suitable size for the crypt. Each crypt is designed for one interment unless special request is made for multiple interments and approved by the Columbarium Board. No other restriction is imposed, except the usual bounds of good taste, and except that the names and dates of birth and death shall be marked or placed within the container. St. Peter's reserves the right to reject a container which, in its judgment, will not meet these requirements.

9. A representative of St. Peter's shall be present and shall supervise each interment.

10. Names and birth and death dates of any persons whose remains are interred may be placed on a crypt cover purchased by Buyer to specifications established by St. Peter's. No other information is permitted. Size, type, and manner of lettering will be determined by St. Peter's.

11. Flowers, planting, or other ornamentations are not permitted over crypt in columbarium area, except one arrangement of natural flowers is allowed on the day of interment and on each succeeding All Saint's Day (November 1st) subject to the approval of the clergy.

12. St. Peter's will arrange for the opening and closing of the individual crypt at the time of interment; such cost will be borne by the Buyer.

13. St. Peter's will endeavor to protect all containers deposited in the columbarium facilities, assuming such responsibility with respect to them as it affords its own property. St. Peter's shall NOT BE LIABLE for destruction resulting from vandalism, terrorism, or natural disaster. Any and all liability that St. Peter's may be found to have shall be limited to the cost of replacement and repair of property damages and shall not extend to mental anguish and/or pain and suffering of the heirs, members of the estate, and/or family of any individual interred.

14. Interred remains may be removed from the crypt with the written consent of St. Peter's and of the Buyer and spouse of the person interred, or the survivor of them, or, if neither is living, of the personal representative (if any) or the next of kin of the person interred. In any such instance, a receipt must be signed by the party so acting, indemnifying St. Peter's against all liability. No refunds are granted under any circumstances. Ashes interred in the common crypt may be removed under such conditions as St. Peter's may from time to time impose.

15. In the event that the present church facilities are demolished or the ownership of the church property is transferred by the church, or the columbarium facilities are discontinued, (a) the right to inter shall

terminate without any refund to existing subscribers, (b) the vestry or its designee or successor shall exercise maximum effort to locate and notify surviving heirs and afford them the opportunity to remove the containers, (c) in the event a container is not removed by the heirs, St. Peter's shall have the right to remove and dispose of it in such a manner as it shall deem proper, and (d) in the event the parish is moved to a different location, the vestry shall make every reasonable effort to provide facilities comparable to those then existing for the redepositing of the containers committed to its care, and the vestry shall exercise maximum effort to locate and notify surviving heirs of the new locations.

16. Ordinarily, a Buyer shall be a canonical member of the mission of St. Peter's and all designees should be limited to those related by the kinship or marriage. However, St. Peter's, in its sole discretion, may accept those not canonical members of the congregation for interment.

17. The responsibility of all records relative to the use of the columbarium facilities rests with the vestry or its designee.

18. No individual vicar of St. Peter's Episcopal Church, no individual members of the vestry, and no individual or member of a Board designated to maintain or supervise the columbarium facilities shall be personally liable for any damage or for the defense of any claim of damage or for any loss resulting from or to the columbarium facilities, containers, or any interred remains.

19. All services of the funeral and interment are to be from the Episcopal *Book of Common Prayer* conducted by clergy of St. Peter's Episcopal Church or those deputized by them. Either of the rites for the Burial of Dead may be used, or any rite that satisfies the following form.

AN ORDER FOR BURIAL

When, for pastoral considerations, neither of the burial rites in this book is deemed appropriate, the following form is used:

1. The body is received. The celebrant may meet the body and conduct it into the church or chapel, or it may be in place before the congregation assembles.

2. Anthems from Holy Scripture or Psalms may be sung or said, or a hymn may be sung.

3. Prayer may be offered for the bereaved.

4. One or more passages of Holy Scripture are read. Psalms, hymns, or anthems may follow the readings. If there is to be a Communion, the last reading is from the Gospel.

5. A homily may follow the readings, and the Apostles' Creed may be recited.

6. Prayer, including the Lord's Prayer, is offered for the deceased, for those who mourn, and for the Christian community, remembering the promises of God in Christ about eternal life.

7. The deceased is commended to God, and the body is committed to its resting place. The committal may take place either when the preceding service has been held or at the graveside.

8. If there is a Communion, it precedes the commendation, and begins with the Peace and Offertory of the Eucharist. Any of the authorized eucharistic prayers may be used.

APPENDIX 4. A FORM OF PRAYER AT A TIME WHEN LIFE-SUSTAINING
TREATMENT IS WITHDRAWN*

Committee on Medical Ethics, Diocese of Washington, Washington, D.C.

CONCERNING THE SERVICE

This service may be used when family, friends, and caregivers join together
for prayer with someone from whom life-sustaining treatment is to be
withdrawn. It commends this person to God at a solemn time when the
limits of human ability to reverse his or her course toward death are
acknowledged. The service is appropriate for situations in which death is
expected to follow soon after the withdrawal of treatment. Should death
be expected immediately after, some may prefer to use the service of
Ministration at the Time of Death, adding some of the collects and readings from this service.

If Communion is desired, this service may constitute the Liturgy of
the Word. The service then continues with one of the Eucharistic Prayers
from *The Book of Common Prayer.* If Communion under Special
Circumstances is used, the celebrant may read one of the Gospel passages
appointed in that service and continue immediately with the Peace, the
Lord's Prayer, and the administration of the Sacrament.

When there is no Communion, the officiant may be clerical or lay. In
either case, another person may be incited to read the lessons. The readings and prayers should be adapted to the needs of those present.

The service may be held either at the bedside of the person from
whom treatment is to be withdrawn or apart from him or her, and it may
be used whether the person is conscious or unconscious.

> Diocese of Washington
> Church House
> Mount Saint Alban
> Washington, D.C. 20016
> (202)537-6555

*Reprinted with permission from Committee on Medical Ethics, Diocese of Washington,
*Before You Need Them: Advance Directives for Health Care, Living Wills and Durable Powers of
Attorney* (Cincinnati, Ohio: Forward Movement Publications, 1995), 31–39.

A Form of Prayer at a Time When Life-Sustaining Treatment Is Withdrawn

The Officiant begins the service, the people gathered around the bedside or in another setting, with the following sentence.

The Lamb at the center of the throne will be their shepherd, and he will guide them to springs of the water of life, and God will wipe away every tear from their eyes. *Revelation 7:17*

THE COLLECT

The Officiant says to the people	The Lord be with you.
People	And also with you.
Celebrant	Let us pray.

The Officiant says

O God, our Creator and Sustainer, receive our prayers on behalf of your servant N. We thank you for the love and companionship we have shared with him/her. Give us grace now to accept the limits of human healing as we commend N. into your merciful care. Strengthen us, we pray, in this time of trial and help us to continue to serve and care for one another, through Jesus Christ, our Savior.

People	Amen.

THE LESSONS

The Reader says	A Reading from the Letter of Paul to the Romans *(or 1 Corinthians 15:51–57 may be read instead).*

Who will separate us from the love of Christ? Will hardship, or distress, or persecution, or famine, or nakedness, or peril, or sword?

For I am convinced that neither death, nor life, nor angels, nor rulers, nor things present, nor things to come, nor powers, nor height, nor depth, nor anything else in all creation, will be able to separate us from the love of God in Christ Jesus our Lord. *(Romans 8:35, 38–39)*

The Reader says	The Word of the Lord.
People	Thanks be to God.

Silence may follow.

Those present may wish to say the Psalm responsively.

The Reader says   The Twenty-third Psalm
                                          (Or Psalm 103 may be read instead)

The Lord is my shepherd;*
  I shall not want.
He maketh me to lie down in green pastures;*
  he leadeth me beside still waters.
He restoreth my soul;*
  he leadeth me in the paths of righteousness for his Name's sake.
Yea, though I walk through the valley of the shadow of death, I will fear no evil;*
  for thou art with me;
  thy rod and thy staff, they comfort me.
Thou preparest a table before me in the presence of mine enemies;*
  Thou anointest my head with oil;
  my cup runneth over.
Surely goodness and mercy shall follow me all the days of my life;*
  And I will dwell in the house of the Lord for ever.

THE GOSPEL

The Deacon or Minister appointed reads the Gospel, first saying

A Reading (lesson) from the Gospel of John.

Do not let your hearts be troubled. Believe in God, believe also in me. In my Father's house there are many dwelling places. If it were not so, would I have told you that I go to prepare a place for you? And if I go and prepare a place for you, I will come again and will take you to myself, so that where I am, there you may be also. *(John 14:1–3)*

At the end of the Gospel, the Reader says
                                          The Word of the Lord.

People   Thanks be to God.

THE PRAYERS

Officiant	The Lord be with you.
People	And also with you.
Officiant	Let us pray.
Officiant and people	Our Father, who art in heaven,

        hallowed be thy Name,
        thy kingdom come,
        thy will be done,
            on earth as it is in heaven.
Give us this day our daily bread.
And forgive us our trespasses,
        as we forgive those
            who trespass against us.
And lead us not into temptation,
        but deliver us from evil.
For thine is the kingdom,
        and the power, and the glory,
            for ever and ever. Amen.

or

Our Father in heaven,
        hallowed be your Name.
        your kingdom come,
        your will be done,
            on earth as in heaven.
Give us today our daily bread.
Forgive us our sins
        as we forgive those
            who sin against us.
Save us from the time of trial,
        and deliver us from evil.
For the kingdom, the power,
        and the glory are yours,
            now and for ever. Amen.

SUGGESTED COLLECTS

A Collect for Medical and Nursing Caregivers
    O God, our Healer and Redeemer, we thank you for the compassion-
ate medical and nursing care N. has received. Bless these and all doctors
and nurses; fill them with knowledge, understanding, virtue, and patience;
and strengthen them as they return to their ministry of healing and comforting; through Jesus Christ our Lord. Amen.

A Collect for All Who Suffer
    O God, our Creator, look with compassion on all who suffer and heal
their spirits, that they may be released from the bondage of sickness and
fear. Care for the desolate, give rest to the weary, comfort the sorrowful,
bless the dying and bring them in peace and safety to your Paradise of love;
through Jesus Christ, our Lord. Amen.

A Collect for One from Whom Treatment Is to Be Withdrawn
    Dear Heavenly Creator, whose peace passes all understanding, we pray
that when you deem it time you will free your servant N. from all earthly
cares, pardon his/her sins, release him/her from pain and suffering, and
grant that he/she may come to dwell with all your saints in everlasting joy;
through Jesus Christ our Lord. Amen.

*Silence may be kept, and free intercessions, thanksgivings, and other prayers
may be offered.*

*The Officiant may lay hands on the person from whom treatment is to be
withdrawn and say one of the following:*

N., I lay my hands upon you in the Name of our Lord and Savior, Jesus
Christ, beseeching him to uphold you and fill you with grace, that you may
know the healing power of his love. Amen.

or this:

N., I lay my hands upon you in the Name of the Father, and of the Son, and
of the Holy Spirit, trusting that God will do better things for you than we
can desire or pray for. Amen.

When there is no Communion, the Officiant may conclude with the following:

    The grace of our Lord Jesus Christ, and the love of God, and the fel-
lowship of the Holy Spirit, be with us all evermore. Amen. *(2 Corinthians
13:14)*

or this:

Glory to God whose power, working in us, can do infinitely more than we can ask or imagine; Glory to him from generation to generation in the Church, and in Christ Jesus for ever and ever. Amen. *(Ephesians 3:20, 21)*

A blessing may be given here if a bishop or priest is present.

MEMBERS OF END OF LIFE TASK FORCE

Cynthia B. Cohen, Ph.D., J.D., Chair, Senior Research Fellow, Kennedy Institute of Ethics, Georgetown University, Washington, D.C.

The Rev. Randolph K. Dales, Rector, All Saints' Church, Wolfeboro, New Hampshire

The Rev. Jan C. Heller, Ph.D., System Director, Office of Ethics and Theology, Providence Health System, Seattle, Washington

Bruce Jennings, Executive Vice President, The Hastings Center, Garrison, New York

Margaret E. Mohrmann, M.D., Ph.D., Associate Professor of Pediatrics and Medical Education, University of Virginia Medical Center, Charlottesville, Virginia

The Rev. E. F. Michael Morgan, Ph.D., Rector, Church of the Good Shepherd, Athens, Ohio

The Rt. Rev. Kenneth L. Price, D.D., Suffragan Bishop, Diocese of Southern Ohio, Columbus, Ohio

The Rev. David A. Scott, Ph.D., William Meade Professor of Theology and Ethics, Virginia Theological Seminary, Alexandria, Virginia

Timothy F. Sedgwick, Ph.D., Professor of Christian Ethics, Virginia Theological Seminary, Alexandria, Virginia

David H. Smith, Ph.D., Director, The Poynter Center for the Study of Ethics and American Institutions, Indiana University, Bloomington, Indiana

Karen Roberts Turner, J.D., M.A., Principal, Montedonico, Hamilton, and Altman, Chevy Chase, Maryland